the Signs of our SAVIOUR

TIM CHRISTOSON & TERRIE CHAPPELL

Copyright © 2009 by Striving Together Publications. All Scripture quotations are taken from the King James Version.

First published in 2009 by Striving Together Publications, a ministry of Lancaster Baptist Church, Lancaster, CA 93535. Striving Together Publications is committed to providing tried, trusted, and proven books that will further equip local churches to carry out the Great Commission. Your comments and suggestions are valued.

All rights reserved. No part of this book may be reproduced, stored in a retrieval system, or transmitted in any form or by any means—electronic, mechanical, photocopy, recording, or otherwise—without written permission of the publisher, except that which is designated or for brief quotations in printed reviews.

Striving Together Publications
4020 E. Lancaster Blvd.
Lancaster, CA 93535
800.201.7748

Edited by Danielle Mordh
Cover design by Andrew Jones
Layout by Craig Parker

ISBN 978-1-59894-084-8
Printed in Canada

Contents

How to Use This Curriculum 5

Lesson One—Jesus Turns Water into Wine 10

Lesson Two—Jesus Heals a Son 22

Lesson Three—Jesus Helps Peter Catch Fish 36

Lesson Four—Jesus Heals a Friend 48

Lesson Five—Jesus Raises the Widow's Son 60

Lesson Six—Jesus Calms the Storm 72

Lesson Seven—Jesus Sets a Maniac Free 84

Lesson Eight—Jesus Heals a Sick Woman 96

Lesson Nine—Jesus Feeds Five Thousand 108

Lesson Ten—Jesus Walks on Water 120

Lesson Eleven—Jesus Heals a Blind Man 132

Lesson Twelve—Jesus Heals Ten Lepers 144

Lesson Thirteen—Jesus Raises His Friend Lazarus 156

How to Use This Curriculum

A Series of Thirteen Lessons

This curriculum series, *The Signs of Our Saviour*, focuses on thirteen miracles performed by our Lord Jesus Christ during His earthly ministry. These miracles are studied in chronological order and are taken from all four of the Gospel records.

The Life of Christ

This series is part of a larger, four-quarter, fifty-two lesson series on the life of Christ. The other three series include *The Stories of Our Saviour*, which focuses on our Lord's parables, *The Steps of Our Saviour*, which focuses on the events which occurred early in Jesus' earthly ministry, and *The Sacrifice of Our Saviour*, which focuses on the betrayal, crucifixion, resurrection, and ascension of Christ.

Class Time

Each lesson contains sufficient resources to fill a ninety minute class period. For those attempting to use the curriculum for a sixty minute class period, we suggest the teacher choose which resources would be most effective and use them accordingly.

Age Appropriateness

This curriculum and its accompanying resources have been written for use with elementary-age children. Those who teach preschool-age children will also find it compatible for use with ages four and under.

Ideas & Resources Included

Experts suggest that we can estimate the average child's attention span as one minute per year of life. So for example, those teaching eight-year-olds should expect to change activities in the classroom every eight minutes or so, in order to keep the students' attention. The one exception to this rule would be the main Bible lesson itself. During the Bible lesson, attention can be kept through the combined use of visual aids such as flash cards, objects, role-play, digital projection, and a chalk/dry-erase board.

The Signs of Our Saviour | © 2009 Striving Together Publications

Included in Every Lesson:

One-Page Lesson Snapshot
At the beginning of each lesson is a summary page, intended to be photocopied by the teacher and tucked into his or her Bible for ready reference. This page may also be distributed to the assistant teachers in advance, so they may prepare for their classroom responsibilities. This page includes each week's lesson title, Scripture references, memory verse, lesson outline, and a suggested class schedule.

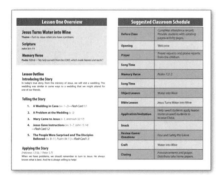

Scripture Passage
Great teaching begins with God's Word! Teachers should study the included Scripture passage numerous times throughout the week, make notes, and become familiar with the passage.

Teacher's Checklist
Use the weekly checklist to gather the appropriate materials in preparation for Sunday. Instructions may be given to an assistant teacher to pick up the needed items for the suggested craft, snack, game, or object lesson. The checklist identifies additional items found on the Ministry Resource CD (sold separately).

Snack Suggestion
Children will enjoy a different snack each week, which will not only be a treat but also a reminder of the truth learned. This is a fun and tasty way to give children a break during their time in the classroom.

Lesson Introduction
As each week's lesson begins, thought-provoking questions are asked, as students consider their own real-life circumstances, similar to those they will encounter in the Scripture. As you enter the lesson, allow for a brief period of answers and open discussion.

Verse-by-Verse Bible Lesson
Each lesson surveys a select portion of Scripture taking a walk of discovery through the biblical record. Lessons are divided into five easy-to-identify points with helpful cross references included.

Lesson Application
At the conclusion of each lesson, the teacher should seek to remind students of one or two primary truths to take away from the story. Then ask, in practical terms, how children might apply those truths during the week. At this time in the lesson, students who would like to receive Christ as Saviour should be encouraged to speak to a trained counselor.

Review Game with Questions
A unique theme-oriented game is included in each lesson for the purpose of review. While other questions may be added by the teacher, a list of initial review questions designed to reinforce the lesson are provided for use during the game.

Teaching the Memory Verse
A creative way of teaching the week's memory verse is included in each lesson. The Visual Resource Packet (sold separately) includes visuals for use with each memory verse. These visuals are also available on the Ministry Resource CD (sold separately).

Object Lesson
Children will remember the five-minute object lessons designed to support the Bible lesson. Each object lesson is easy to teach and simple to prepare using objects most of us have at home or that are available at a retail store.

Craft
Each lesson includes a craft that students and parents will enjoy putting on display! The craft section includes a supply list, easy-to-follow directions, and simple thoughts on how it relates to the Bible lesson.

Teaching Tips
Creative ideas and suggestions are provided for the purpose of effectively delivering the truths contained in each week's lesson.

Teacher's Note
Historical notes, practical instructions, and biblical definitions are provided to assist the teacher in study and preparation.

Suggested Visual Aids:

The "mixing up" of the weekly visuals will keep students engaged and will prevent predictability.

Flash Cards
In four of the thirteen lessons, flash cards are used to illustrate the Bible story (three cards for each selected story). Find the icon in the lesson margin to show the flash card to the students at the appropriate time. These twelve flash cards are included in the Visual Resource Packet (sold separately).

Act It Out
In certain lessons, we suggest selecting students to help "act out" the Bible story. Vary your choices in order to give all students who wish to be involved the opportunity to do so throughout the course of the series. The students more eager to participate in this role play are likely those who will benefit most from the exercise.

Draw It!
Many classrooms are equipped with a chalk or dry-erase marker board. Included in the margin of select lessons are simple sketches that even the most artistically-challenged teacher can draw! We suggest that you have the students draw along with you to reinforce the events taking place in the story.

Use an Object
Some weeks, teachers may utilize a physical object to keep students' attention. Suggested props of this nature are found at strategic points in the margin of the Bible lesson.

The Ministry Resource CD:
We recommend that each church or class purchase the Ministry Resource CD and make the files available to as many teachers as desired. This enables the investment in the CD to be spread over an unlimited volume and time.

Coloring Pages
Younger children (roughly three-year-olds through 3rd grade) will enjoy coloring a scene from each week's Bible lesson. Share an original copy with each teacher and provide as many photocopies as needed for all classes, one per student.

Activity Pages

Older children (roughly 3rd through 6th grades) will enjoy creative activities related to each week's Bible lesson. Activities include word searches, crossword puzzles, mazes, and brainteasers. Share an original copy with each teacher and provide as many photocopies as needed for all classes, one per student.

Student Take-Home Paper

The take-home paper is designed to help students take the Bible truth into the week ahead as they leave the classroom. Take-home papers will remind students of the weekly memory verse, include additional review questions, and suggest practical ways for applying the lesson in everyday experiences. Share an original copy with each teacher and provide as many photocopies as needed for all classes, one per student.

PowerPoint Presentation

A Microsoft PowerPoint presentation is available for each of the thirteen lessons. If you have a television, computer monitor, or projector available, children will enjoy being able to follow the main points of the lesson on the screen. Each week's memory verse is also included in the presentation. These presentations are fully editable, and may be shared with as many teachers as desired. Feel free to move the PowerPoint files from the CD to your own computer, and to add or edit slides as you wish.

Memory Verse Visuals

The same visuals included in the Visual Resource Packet are included in PDF form on the Ministry Resource CD. These are provided so that teachers may use the images in projection or another form, including providing copies to students.

Craft and Game Templates

Throughout the series, templates are utilized with select crafts and games. These templates are found on the Ministry Resource CD in PDF form.

Suggested Classroom Schedule

Before Class	Complete attendance record. Provide students with coloring pages/activity pages.
Opening	Welcome
Prayer	Prayer requests and praise reports from the children
Song Time	
Memory Verse	Psalm 121:2
Song Time	
Object Lesson	Water into Wine
Bible Lesson	Jesus Turns Water into Wine
Application/Invitation	Help saved students apply lesson. Invite unsaved students to receive Christ.
Snack	Wedding Cupcakes
Review Game/ Questions	Rice and Safety Pin Game
Craft	Water into Wine
Closing	Announcements and Prayer Distribute take-home papers.

Lesson One Overview

Jesus Turns Water into Wine

Theme—Turn to Jesus when you have a problem.

Scripture
John 2:1–11

Memory Verse
Psalm 121:2—"My help cometh from the LORD, which made heaven and earth."

Lesson Outline
Introducing the Story
In today's true story, from the ministry of Jesus, we will visit a wedding. This wedding was similar in some ways to a wedding that we might attend for one of our friends.

Telling the Story
1. **A Wedding in Cana** (vv. 1–2)

2. **A Problem at the Wedding** (v. 3)

3. **Mary Came to Jesus** (v. 3, Jeremiah 32:17)—Flash Card 1.1

4. **Jesus Gave Instructions** (vv. 5–7, John 15:14) —Flash Card 1.2

5. **The People Were Surprised and the Disciples Believed** (vv. 8–11, Psalm 84:11)—Flash Card 1.3

Applying the Story
(Hebrews 13:5b, 1 Peter 5:7)
When we have problems, we should remember to turn to Jesus. He always knows what is best, and He is always willing to help!

1 Lesson One

Jesus Turns Water into Wine

Theme: Turn to Jesus when you have a problem.

Scripture

Memory Verse

Psalm 121:2
"My help cometh from the LORD, which made heaven and earth."

John 2:1–11

1   And the third day there was a marriage in Cana of Galilee; and the mother of Jesus was there:
2   And both Jesus was called, and his disciples, to the marriage.
3   And when they wanted wine, the mother of Jesus saith unto him, They have no wine.
4   Jesus saith unto her, Woman, what have I to do with thee? mine hour is not yet come.
5   His mother saith unto the servants, Whatsoever he saith unto you, do it.
6   And there were set there six waterpots of stone, after the manner of the purifying of the Jews, containing two or three firkins apiece.
7   Jesus saith unto them, Fill the waterpots with water. And they filled them up to the brim.
8   And he saith unto them, Draw out now, and bear unto the governor of the feast. And they bare it.
9   When the ruler of the feast had tasted the water that was made wine, and knew not whence it was: (but the servants which drew the water knew;) the governor of the feast called the bridegroom,
10 And saith unto him, Every man at the beginning doth set forth good wine; and when men have well drunk, then that which is worse: but thou hast kept the good wine until now.
11 This beginning of miracles did Jesus in Cana of Galilee, and manifested forth his glory; and his disciples believed on him.

Lesson One—Jesus Turns Water into Wine

Teacher's Checklist

- Read John 2:1–11 daily
- Study Lesson One
- Prepare snack—white cupcakes and grape punch (or you may use the craft idea as beverage)
- Flashcards 1.1–1.3
- Gather for object lesson—gallon of water, red food coloring, and a pitcher
- Gather for game—a bowl of uncooked rice, small gold safety pins
- Memory verse flashcards for Psalm 121:2 (3 flashcards)
- Purchase for craft—sixteen ounce bottles of water (one per student)
- Purchase for craft—individual drink mix packets for water bottles (one per student)
- Print bottle labels using template from the Ministry Resource CD (one per student)
- Tape and scissors (for craft)
- Print and duplicate Coloring Pages or Activity Pages on the Ministry Resource CD (one per student)
- Print and duplicate Take-Home Paper on the Ministry Resource CD (one per student)

Serve "wedding" cupcakes.

Lesson One—Jesus Turns Water into Wine

Bible Lesson

Scripture: John 2:1–11

INTRODUCING THE STORY

Have you ever been to the wedding of a friend or relative? Weddings are happy occasions! Everyone is excited for the young man and the young woman who love one another and who are beginning their own family together. It's one of the most special days in a person's life!

Preparing for a wedding can be a lot of work! The bride, the groom, and their family members want everything to be just right—the dresses, the flowers, the music, the ceremony, and more.

What was your favorite part of a wedding that you attended? After the wedding, did you attend a party or dinner (we sometimes call them a reception)? Was there a giant cake? Did the bride and groom feed one another a piece of the cake? If so, were they kind when they fed one another?

In today's true story from the ministry of Jesus, we will visit a wedding. This wedding was similar in some ways to a wedding that we might attend today for one of our friends.

> **Teaching Tip**
>
> In an all girls class, play a quick bridal shower game at the beginning of class.

THE STORY

1. A Wedding in Cana (vv.1–2)

When Jesus preached and taught during His time on earth, He did much of this work in an area called Galilee. In spite of its name, the Sea of Galilee is really about as large as a good-sized lake (about eight miles across and about thirteen miles long). It was larger than many lakes you have probably seen but still about half the size of Lake Tahoe, for example. It was in the cities around this lake that Jesus met and called most of His disciples. Cana was a small town not far from the Sea of Galilee.

In this village of Cana, a young couple was getting married. Not only was Jesus invited to the wedding, but His mother, Mary, was also invited along with several of His disciples. I'm sure Jesus was happy for this young couple! I would imagine the people at the wedding enjoyed talking with

Lesson One—Jesus Turns Water into Wine

Teacher's Note

For further reading on the New Testament's teaching concerning alcohol and the biblical use of the term *wine*, see the book available from Striving Together Publications, *Discerning Alcohol*, by Paul Chappell.

Jesus and being around Him. By being at the wedding, Jesus showed that He considered the relationship between a husband and wife to be very special.

2. A Problem at the Wedding (v. 3)

During the meal, there was a problem—the people ran out of wine to drink! The Bible uses the word *wine*, which literally means, "that which comes from grapes." In Bible times, people used the word *wine* to describe any drink or substance that came from grapes—including grape juice, grape jelly, and even the grapes themselves. What Jesus made was not the same kind of drink that people call wine today—the Bible says that we should avoid that kind of wine (Proverbs 20:1, 23:29–35). We are not sure why they ran out of wine—or grape juice—at this wedding. Maybe someone was asked to bring some, and he forgot. Or maybe more people attended the wedding than they had expected. Either way, this was a problem!

Can you imagine sinking your teeth into a delicious piece of cake, complete with sugary frosting, only to find out moments later that there was nothing to drink? What's more, this wedding not only had cake to eat, but the Bible says they enjoyed an entire feast (v. 8b)!

Flash Card 1.1

3. Mary Came to Jesus (v. 3)

No one at the wedding knew Jesus better than His mother, Mary. As soon as she heard about the problem, she told Jesus knowing that He could help. Mary may have been a close friend of this family, having volunteered to help them with the wedding feast.

Even though at this point in His life, Jesus had not yet performed any miracles, Mary believed in His power. Do you think Jesus could solve this problem? Do you think there are any problems too hard for Him to solve?

> **Jeremiah 32:17**
> 17 Ah Lord GOD! behold, thou hast made the heaven and the earth by thy great power and stretched out arm, and there is nothing too hard for thee:

Jesus was not only able to help, but also willing to help—He always is! When some people have problems, they ask people around them for help but forget to ask Jesus for help. Other people might even get upset and blame Jesus for their problem. Mary did the right thing and came to the right Person! She did not go to the man in charge of the meal. She did not go to the bride, the groom, or their family members. She did not go to the disciples. She went directly to Jesus with her problem.

4. Jesus Gave Instructions (vv. 5–7)

Mary said something very interesting to the people helping at the wedding, "Whatsoever he saith unto you, do it" (verse 5). Isn't that good advice?

Children, you will always be glad whenever you do what Jesus says! If Jesus says something to us in His Book, the Bible, we should obey it. What are some things Jesus has told us we should do? He has told us to be kind (Ephesians 4:31–32), to forgive people (Colossians 3:13), to tell the truth (Ephesians 4:15, 25), and more.

Later in His ministry, many days after this story, Jesus reminded His disciples of the importance of following His instructions:

John 15:14
14 Ye are my friends, if ye do whatsoever I command you.

What did Jesus tell these servants to do?

Nearby were six large pots, made of clay or stone, to hold the water people would use for washing their hands (verse 6). During the times of Jesus, many people did not stop to wash their hands before they ate their meal. But for the Jewish people, this was very important. (Have your parents ever explained how important it is to wash your hands before you eat?)

Jesus told the servants to fill these pots with water. They may have wondered why Jesus told them to do this. But instead of asking questions or arguing, they followed His instructions.

We should also remember this lesson when our parents or teachers ask us to do something we don't understand. Jesus always knows best, even when we sometimes don't understand. And He also gives wisdom to

Flash Card 1.2

parents, pastors, and godly teachers. Sometimes we don't like having to follow instructions. But Jesus gave these adults to us because He knew we would need their help. And sometimes that means following their instructions.

We will learn from this story that, when we obey Jesus, He has blessings waiting for us!

After the servants had filled the pots with water, all the way up to the top (verse 7), Jesus instructed them to pour it into the cups of the guests. The servants then watched in amazement as they poured wine out of the pots they had just filled with water.

Flash Card 1.3

5. The People Were Surprised and the Disciples Believed (vv. 8–11)

The Bible tells us about the response of the governor (or ruler) of the feast. This is the man who was in charge of the meal—we might call him a caterer or head-waiter today. He was quite surprised (verses 9–10)! He was not aware of the miracle, at least at first. But when he tasted the wine, he said it was the best that had been served. I'm sure all of the guests were thankful for what Jesus provided.

As you grow up and keep living for the Lord Jesus, you will find that He often surprises you with blessings you did not know He had in store. Jesus wants to bless your life and provide even simple blessings, like delicious food and drinks. We enjoy His blessings, as we allow Him to be present in our lives through staying in church, reading His Word, praying, and following His instructions.

Psalm 84:11

11   For the LORD God is a sun and shield: the LORD will give grace and glory: no good thing will he withhold from them that walk uprightly.

The disciples saw what happened, and the Bible tells us that it helped them to believe in Jesus, even more than they had already (verse 11b). When God does good things for us, it should remind us of His power and love, so we never stop believing that not only is He great, but He is also good.

APPLYING THE STORY

It's a good thing Jesus was at this wedding! If He had not been there, no one would have enjoyed the delicious wine. If you have asked Jesus to be your Saviour, He is always with you. You are never alone!

Hebrews 13:5b

5   …he hath said, I will never leave thee, nor forsake thee.

Sometimes we have problems, like Mary had on this day, and we do not know how to solve them. Maybe we are concerned about a friend or family member's doctor appointment. Maybe we hear that our dad or mom might lose their job. Maybe someone is unkind to us, and we are not sure how to respond.

When we have any of these or other problems, we should remember to turn to Jesus. He always knows what is best. And He is always willing to help!

Instead of trying to figure out how to solve a problem on our own, how can we turn to Jesus, instead?

- By spending time in prayer, asking God to help solve our problem
- By looking for a Bible verse that talks about our problem
- By asking a godly adult, like our Sunday school teacher, if he or she will pray for us or suggest a Bible verse that talks about our problem
- By listening to our pastor or teacher, to see if God may give us answers on how to deal with our problem during a sermon or Bible lesson

You've learned that Jesus is a problem-solver! He has taken care of the greatest problem mankind has—the problem of how a sinful person can go to a perfect, righteous Heaven. He died on the Cross in order that we could be forgiven, and He rose again that His life (a gift to us) could take us to Heaven. (Teacher, explain the Gospel to class.)

1 Peter 5:7

7   Casting all your care upon him; for he careth for you.

Lesson One—Jesus Turns Water into Wine

 **Review Game/ Questions**

Rice and Safety Pin Game

Put tiny safety pins in a bowl of uncooked long grain rice (do not use a clear bowl). Ask a review question. When a student answers correctly, allow that student to put his hand in the bowl without looking and pick out as many safety pins as he can in an allotted time. The student or team with the most safety pins wins the game.

1. What special event took place in today's lesson?
   Answer: Wedding

2. Where did the wedding take place?
   Answer: Cana, near the Sea of Galilee

3. Who attended the wedding feast?
   Answer: Mary, the mother of Jesus, Jesus and the disciples

4. What did they run out of at the feast?
   Answer: Wine

5. Who did Mary ask to take care of the problem?
   Answer: Jesus

6. What did Jesus tell the servants to do?
   Answer: Fill six large stone jars with water.

7. What did the disciples do when they saw Jesus' miracle?
   Answer: Believed in Him

8. How did Jesus solve the greatest problem man has ever had?
   Answer: He died on the Cross and rose again so our sins could be forgiven.

9. What should you do when you have a problem this week?
   Answer: Tell God about it, and trust Him to help you.

Lesson One—Jesus Turns Water into Wine

Teaching the Memory Verse

Psalm 121:2

2 *My help cometh from the LORD, which made heaven and earth.*

Who do you turn to when you have a problem? (parents, friends, pastor, teachers). I am so glad God gave us parents, our pastor, teachers, and police officers to help us when we have a problem. But there are times when we feel like no one is there to help us, our problem is so big, or maybe no one is listening to us. The Bible teaches us that there IS someone we can always trust to help us with any problem we face!

Open your Bible to Psalm 121:2. Read verse together.

Explain that the reference tells us *where the verse lives* in the Bible. It is the *address* of the verse.

"My help"—The Bible tells us we all need help. We need to recognize that sometimes we need help.

"cometh from the LORD"—The world wants to help us with our problems but the world's help is not always good or right. Sometimes we think we can handle it all by ourselves. But God wants us to turn to Him for help.

"which made heaven and earth"—Maybe you've said this little phrase with kids at school: "My dad is stronger than your dad!" Well, our Heavenly Father is better than help we find anywhere or in anyone else. He made Heaven and earth. If He can do that, He is able to help us through any problem we face.

Use companion flashcards found in Visual Resource Packet or images found on the Ministry Resource CD.

The Signs of Our Saviour | © 2009 Striving Together Publications

Lesson One—Jesus Turns Water into Wine

Object Lesson—Water into Wine

Objects needed:
Bring in a clear pitcher that has red food coloring in the bottom. Pour clean water from a gallon jug and let the students see the water turn red.

Craft—Water into Wine

Getting It Together

Per student:
1   Unopened bottle of water
1   Individual drink mix packet for water bottles
1   Water bottle label located on the Ministry Resource CD
Tape
Scissors

Putting It Together

1. Remove the previous water bottle label.
2. Color the water bottle label.
3. Tape the verse template label around the water bottle.
4. Poor the drink mix into the water.

Seeing It Together

This water bottle can help us remember that Jesus turned the water into wine! It will also remind us that we can turn to Jesus whenever we have a problem. (Ask students to name some problems they may have in life, and explain how they can turn to Jesus in each of those situations.)

Teaching Tip

You may want to give each student an individual drink mix packet (such as is available from *Crystal Light*) to use with their water bottles.

20 | The Signs of Our Saviour | © 2009 Striving Together Publications

Lesson One—Jesus Turns Water into Wine

 ## Additional Resources

Find the following items on the Ministry Resource CD:
- Coloring Page (for younger children)
- Activity Page (for older children)
- Student Take-Home Paper
- PowerPoint Presentation

Suggested Classroom Schedule

Before Class	Complete attendance record. Provide students with coloring pages/activity pages.
Opening	Welcome
Prayer	Prayer requests and praise reports from the children
Song Time	
Memory Verses	Proverbs 3:5–6
Song Time	
Object Lesson	Trust Me!
Bible Lesson	Jesus Heals a Son
Application/Invitation	Help saved students apply lesson. Invite unsaved students to receive Christ.
Snack	
Review Game/ Questions	True/False Relay
Craft	Time to Believe
Closing	Announcements and Prayer Distribute take-home papers.

Lesson Two Overview

Jesus Heals a Son

Theme—We can believe what Jesus says.

Scripture
John 4:46–54

Memory Verses
Proverbs 3:5–6—*"Trust in the LORD with all thine heart; and lean not unto thine own understanding. In all thy ways acknowledge him, and he shall direct thy paths."*

Lesson Outline
Introducing the Story

Today we will meet a man who chose to believe what Jesus told him. He chose to believe the promise that Jesus made, and he was not disappointed!

Telling the Story
1. **A Nobleman's Son Is Very Sick** *(v. 46)*

2. **The Nobleman Believes the Promise of Jesus**
   (vv. 48–50, Numbers 23:19)

3. **Good News from the Servants** *(v. 51)*

4. **An Amazing Discovery** *(vv. 52–54, Isaiah 65:24)*

Applying the Story *(1 Thessalonians 2:13)*
The nobleman did the right thing when he chose to come to Jesus for help for his son. We must also choose to believe what Jesus says. We must have faith in God's Word!

2 Lesson Two

Jesus Heals a Son

Theme: We can believe what Jesus says.

Scripture

John 4:46–54

46   So Jesus came again into Cana of Galilee, where he made the water wine. And there was a certain nobleman, whose son was sick at Capernaum.

47   When he heard that Jesus was come out of Judaea into Galilee, he went unto him, and besought him that he would come down, and heal his son: for he was at the point of death.

48   Then said Jesus unto him, Except ye see signs and wonders, ye will not believe.

49   The nobleman saith unto him, Sir, come down ere my child die.

50   Jesus saith unto him, Go thy way; thy son liveth. And the man believed the word that Jesus had spoken unto him, and he went his way.

51   And as he was now going down, his servants met him, and told him, saying, Thy son liveth.

52   Then enquired he of them the hour when he began to amend. And they said unto him, Yesterday at the seventh hour the fever left him.

53   So the father knew that it was at the same hour, in the which Jesus said unto him, Thy son liveth: and himself believed, and his whole house.

54   This is again the second miracle that Jesus did, when he was come out of Judaea into Galilee.

Memory Verses

Proverbs 3:5–6
"Trust in the LORD with all thine heart; and lean not unto thine own understanding. In all thy ways acknowledge him, and he shall direct thy paths."

Lesson Two—Jesus Heals a Son

Teacher's Checklist

- ❑ Read John 4:46–54 daily
- ❑ Study Lesson Two
- ❑ Gather props for lesson—badge for nobleman, Bible for Jesus, cloth and thermometer for nobleman's sick son, and hand towels or napkins to represent servants
- ❑ Prepare snack—crackers and Sprite
- ❑ Gather materials for object lesson—box mailer, labels, cooked fettuccine, jar with lid, packing tape, blindfolds, and rubber gloves
- ❑ Print True/False cards from the Ministry Resource CD for review game
- ❑ Gather for game—clothespins
- ❑ Memory verse flashcards (Proverbs 3:5–6)
- ❑ Purchase for Craft—Brads
- ❑ Print and duplicate clock template for craft
- ❑ Print and duplicate clock hands for craft
- ❑ Crayons and scissors for craft
- ❑ Print and duplicate Coloring Pages or Activity Pages on the Ministry Resource CD (one per student)
- ❑ Print and duplicate Take-Home Paper on the Ministry Resource CD (one per student)

Snack Suggestion

Serve crackers and Sprite and explain that this is a typical snack for a person who is sick or not feeling well.

Lesson Two—Jesus Heals a Son

Bible Lesson

Scripture: John 4:46–54

INTRODUCING THE STORY

Has anyone ever made a promise to you that they did not keep? Maybe they were unable to keep it. Or maybe they deliberately chose not to keep it.

Maybe a school teacher told you that during recess on a particular day, your class would play an exciting game. But when that day came, it was rainy, and you were required to stay inside for recess. Though it was not the teacher's fault that the promise was not kept, still the experience was disappointing.

Maybe one of your parents intended to take you to an interesting place for some time of family fun. But on the way, your family got lost! I'm sure whoever was driving the car did not intend to get lost, but still there was a promise not kept.

One of the wonderful things about our Saviour, Jesus Christ, is that He will always keep His promises! Hebrews 10:23 simply says about our Lord, "…he is faithful that promised."

When Jesus spoke to people during His earthly ministry, His followers always knew that they could believe what He had said. Jesus has spoken to us today also. He has spoken to us through His Word, the Bible. Do you think we can still believe what He says, as people were able to believe what He said long ago?

Today we will meet a man who chose to believe what Jesus told him. He chose to believe the promise that Jesus made, and he was not disappointed! There are many things during our lives on this earth that we will not understand, and some days will be difficult. But one thing we can know is that if Jesus has made us a promise, He will always keep it!

Teaching Tip

Engage students in acting out today's lesson. Give props (mentioned in the Teacher's Checklist) to students as they act out the story.

THE STORY

1. A Nobleman's Son Is Very Sick (v. 46)

As we have already learned, Jesus did much of His teaching, preaching, healing, and helping near the Sea of Galilee. One of the cities on the coast of the Sea of Galilee was Capernaum. In that city lived a man the Bible calls a

Teacher's Note

Jesus was in Cana, and the nobleman lived in Capernaum (Kuh-purr-nay-uhm). That was about a fifteen mile walk!

The Signs of Our Saviour | © 2009 Striving Together Publications

25

Lesson Two—Jesus Heals a Son

Nobleman
Choose a student to act as a dignitary or important person.

Jesus and Followers
Choose students to represent Jesus and His followers.

Teacher's Note

In verse 49, the nobleman called Jesus, "Sir." Even though he was a man of authority, he submitted to Jesus.

Nobleman's Son
Select a student to lay on the floor with a cloth on his head and perhaps a thermometer under his tongue. (To involve more students, you may also have a servant attending to the sick son.)

nobleman. This means that he was a man of some importance or authority in his community. He may have held some office, like being the mayor of his city.

Being noble brought about special privileges. People would give special treatment and respect to this nobleman because of who he was. It would have been easy for him to find people willing to help him and his family. But this nobleman had so great a problem that no ordinary person could help. He had a terribly ill son. His son was so sick that the Bible says he was very close to death (verse 47).

Sometimes we envy other people who have important jobs or who appear to have many blessings. But we need to remember that even the nobleman had problems he could not solve. No one has so much wealth or respect from others that they do not need Jesus! If professional athletes or famous actresses think that, because they have many things and have people's attention, they do not need Jesus, they are very sadly mistaken!

2. The Nobleman Believes the Promise of Jesus (vv. 48–50)

At first, Jesus tested the nobleman, to see whether he would place his faith in Jesus. He said, in effect, "Will you only believe after I do something spectacular before your eyes?" The nobleman's continued requests demonstrated that he already had faith in who Jesus was. He did not ask Jesus to perform some kind of unusual miracle to prove His power. The nobleman already had faith in His power.

To this faith, Jesus responded by saying, "Go thy way; thy son liveth." The nobleman thought that Jesus could heal his son only if He came in person. But Jesus could perform the miracle of healing from fifteen miles away just by saying the words. The important issue wasn't whether Jesus came to the boy. The important issue was whether the nobleman had faith in Jesus.

When Jesus made this amazing statement, the nobleman had no evidence that the boy was healed. He could only believe Jesus' words. The Bible says, "the man believed the word that Jesus had spoken" (verse 50). This is a simple but wonderful statement about this man. He believed what Jesus said!

You can always believe what God says! See what the Lord had Balaam tell the foolish King Balak:

Numbers 23:19

19 *God is not a man, that he should lie; neither the son of man,*
that he should repent: hath he said, and shall he not do it?
or hath he spoken, and shall he not make it good?

3. Good News from the Servants (v. 51)

Because the nobleman believed what Jesus said—because he had faith in God's Son—he received a wonderful blessing. The man began to make his way back home, but because of how slowly people were able to travel then, he had to stay overnight on the way. I imagine that he lay awake that night wondering if what he believed really could be possible. Would he return home to find his son well? He may have smiled as he fell asleep that night, resting with confidence in who Jesus was.

The next day, on the road to Capernaum, he met his servants (people who worked for the nobleman at his house) coming the opposite way. His servants were happy and excited. They did not know whether he had succeeded in finding Jesus, but they came to bring him the good news that his son was now healed!

Act It Out

Group of Servants
Have a group of students excitedly approach the nobleman.

4. An Amazing Discovery (vv. 52–54)

As the nobleman and his servants celebrated together (do you think they high-fived?), he thought to ask them, "*When* did my son begin to get well?"

They answered that his fever left about the seventh hour (one o'clock in the afternoon, according to the way we keep time today). Have you ever had a fever? The chills and discomfort are miserable! This son had a terrible fever like that, but around one o'clock in the afternoon, he suddenly began to feel better—much better.

Imagine the amazement, as the nobleman asked his servants, "Are you *sure* that's when he began to feel better?"

And they said, "Yes, we're sure. Why?"

And he said, "Because that's *exactly* when Jesus said to me, "Go thy way; thy son liveth."

Teacher's Note

The nobleman had great faith. He believed Jesus, proven by his obedience in returning to his son. Distance was not a hindrance to the power of Jesus! Like the nobleman, we must ask and then continue in obedience, believing our prayers are being answered even though we may not see the answers right away.

Do you think the nobleman or his servants had any question, whether Jesus was the One directly responsible for the boy's healing?

God has told us in His Word that He knows what we need, and He is able to answer our requests *while* we pray and even *before* we pray.

Isaiah 65:24

24 And it shall come to pass, that before they call, I will answer; and while they are yet speaking, I will hear.

Because of this wonderful miracle, the nobleman believed in Jesus. He believed that Jesus was God's Son. Not only did the nobleman believe in Jesus, but also his servants, his son who had been healed, and the rest of his family believed! What a blessing to think of a home where there had been such sadness and grief, where now there was such joy and happiness! That's the difference that Jesus makes! And this family experienced it, because a dad chose to believe what Jesus said.

APPLYING THE STORY

The nobleman did the right thing when he chose to come to Jesus for help for his son. But, do you know what he did next? He did the most important thing! He chose to believe what Jesus said. He had faith in the words of Jesus.

Do you believe what Jesus says? What Jesus has said is contained in His Word, the Bible. The Bible is called the Word of God. Do you believe what God wrote to us in the Bible?

1 Thessalonians 2:13

13 For this cause also thank we God without ceasing, because, when ye received the word of God which ye heard of us, ye received it not as the word of men, but as it is in truth, the word of God, which effectually worketh also in you that believe.

The nobleman showed Jesus his faith in His words when he turned around and headed home, believing that his son was healed. How can we show the Lord our faith in His words?

Lesson Two—Jesus Heals a Son

- By taking time each day to read several verses or chapters in the Bible
- By obeying what we read or are taught from the Bible
- By attending church, where the Bible is preached and taught
- By memorizing verses from the Bible
- By searching what the Bible says concerning areas in life where we have questions

Refer to the resource CD for visual pictures to correspond with the five applications listed to the left.

Lesson Two—Jesus Heals a Son

# Review Game/Questions

True/False Relay

Materials Needed

- a clothespin for each student
- a set of True/False cards for each row (either left to right or front to back)

Instructions

To make the game, print True/False cards from the Ministry Resource CD. You will need one set for each team or row. Cut the 8 ½ x 11 paper into fourths.

Give every student a clothespin, and give students in the back row (or far left side) a set of True/False cards. Ask a true/false question. The student with the card decides if the answer is true or false and then chooses that card.

The student then puts the card on his clothespin and passes it to the person sitting in front of him/her (or to the right of him/her) and that student must grab it with his/her clothespin. No one touches the card with their hands.

Object

The first row that passes the correct answer to the front child wins a point. Continue asking the questions in the same manner. You may want to rotate how the students pass their answer. (If they drop their card they give it back to the first person and begin again.) The row with the most points wins.

1. True or False: This was Jesus' first time to Cana.
   Answer: False (He turned water into wine at the wedding feast.)

2. True or False: A nobleman's son was very sick in Capernaum.
   Answer: True

3. True or False: The nobleman asked Jesus to heal his son before he dies.
   Answer: True

4. True or False: The nobleman asked Jesus five times to come to Capernaum.
   Answer: False (He asked Him only twice.)

5. True or False: Jesus touched the son and healed him.
   Answer: False (Jesus did not go to the son. He just spoke.)

Lesson Two—Jesus Heals a Son

6. True or False: The nobleman believed what Jesus said.
    Answer: True

7. True or False: The servants met the nobleman while he was on his way home.
    Answer: True

8. True or False: When the servants met their master, they said, "Thy son is at the point of death!"
    Answer: False (The servants said, "Thy son liveth!")

9. True or False: The nobleman enquired of them the hour when his son began to mend.
    Answer: True

10. True or False: The boy had been healed the same hour Jesus said he was.
    Answer: True

Lesson Two—Jesus Heals a Son

Teaching the Memory Verses

Proverbs 3:5–6

5 *Trust in the LORD with all thine heart; and lean not unto thine own understanding.*

6 *In all thy ways acknowledge him, and he shall direct thy paths.*

On July 16, 1999, a handsome, wealthy, and successful man (in the world's eyes) "wanted to do it alone". He was flying his single engine airplane over the Atlantic Ocean at night. Rather than trusting his plane's instrument panel he trusted his own instincts instead. Unable to distinguish between the direction of the dark, hazy ocean and the moonless night, he crashed his plane in the Atlantic Ocean, killing himself and his two passengers. (J. F. Kennedy, Jr.)

What a tragic story! Yet, it's just as tragic when we try to live the Christian life on our own rather than trusting our Heavenly Father to guide and direct us.

Open your Bible to Proverbs 3:5–6. Read verses together.

Choose eight students to help hold the flashcards. Call them up one at a time, and explain the visual on each card.

"Trust in the LORD with all thine heart"—Sometimes we don't even think twice about trusting people. We trust pilots, cooks, and sales people, yet we hesitate when it comes to trusting God whole-heartedly.

"and lean not unto thine own understanding"—When we cannot see the "end", keep trusting. Don't fall back into our own way of thinking.

"in all thy ways acknowledge him"—Before making a decision, look to the Lord in prayer and ask Him to give you wisdom.

"and he shall direct thy paths"—God will answer!

Use companion flashcards found in Visual Resource Packet or images found on Ministry Resource CD.

Lesson Two—Jesus Heals a Son

Object Lesson—Trust Me!

Objects needed:
- Box—used for mailing (a good size box is recommended, to grab the students' attention)
- Return label for box—CMSI—Children's Ministry Science Institute.
- Large 'WARNING' label
- Cooked fettuccine noodles (students will eat this so make sure you take care in handling the pasta)
- Jar with screw on lid
- Packing tape
- Blindfolds (approximately 2–4)
- Rubber gloves

Preparation:
Prepare fettuccine noodles. Keep them moistened so they won't dry out. Put noodles in clean glass jar and screw on the lid. Place the jar in the box. You can add some packing peanuts to the box to keep jar stable. Seal box with packing tape and place on the labels.

Arouse Curiosity:
Place the box in a prominent place for all the students to see. When students ask what is in the box, tell them everyone will see what is in the box shortly.

What to say:
Begin telling the class that the Bible is God's Word. It is truth. Continue by saying, "There are many stories in the Bible, and they are all true! Sometimes we read stories that are not true. They are made up. We call theses stories fiction, fables, or old wives tales.

"For example, do you know what a tapeworm is? A tapeworm is a parasite, which means it needs another larger creature to attach to for food. They live in the human or other vertebrae's intestinal system and can survive there for thirty years. Tapeworms are flat, and can get very long, up to thirty-six feet long! When someone has a tapeworm, they lose a lot of weight and get very weak. Once you get a tapeworm it is very hard to get rid of it. The infected person should see a doctor and get medicine.

However, there is an old wives' tale that says you don't need any medicine. It instructs a person who has a tapeworm to fast for a day (so the tapeworm gets hungry and will look for food) and then put buttermilk or heavy cream under the nose. The old wives' tale says that if the person does this, the tapeworm would crawl out of the person's nose! Yuk! Good thing that remedy is just a wives' tale! Aren't you glad we have the truth in the Bible? No wives' tales here!

"Many of you have noticed our package here. It is from Children's Ministry Science Institute and it is addressed to our class."

Put on your rubber gloves. Call on four students to come to the front of class. Put blindfolds on them. As you do that, talk to the kids about trust. Ask them, "Do you trust me? Will you obey me? Would I ask you to do anything that would hurt you? Do you believe me? Good. I am going to ask you do something that requires your trust."

Now open the box (making as much noise as possible). Ask the students to hold out their hands. Unscrew the jar, take a fettuccine noodle, and place it in their hand. Now ask them to eat what is in their hands. This should stir up a reaction from the students, as they should think the noodles are tapeworms.

After a couple of minutes, whether they ate the noodle or not, allow the students to take off the blindfolds. Show them it was just noodles.

Discuss:

What did it take for the students to eat (or why didn't they eat) the noodle? Faith/Trust. "Just as it required faith or trust to eat something when you didn't know what it was, we need to trust our Heavenly Father even when we can't see how He is working in our lives.

We need to believe God and His Word. He would never ask us to do anything that would hurt us. We need to obey the Lord even when we don't see the whole picture.

Lesson Two—Jesus Heals a Son

Craft—Time to Believe

Getting It Together

Per student:
- 1 brass brad
- 1 clock template located on the resource CD
- 1 clock hands template located on the resource CD

Putting It Together

1. Print 1 clock template per student
2. Print and cut the clock hands
3. Color the clock template
4. Attach the clock arms to the center of the clock with 1 brass brad

Seeing It Together

When Jesus said the nobleman's son was healed, the son was healed that very hour! We, too, must take the time to believe and trust God in every trial of our lives! This clock will remind us that we can always believe what Jesus says.

Additional Resources

Find the following items on the Ministry Resource CD:
- Coloring Page (for younger children)
- Activity Page (for older children)
- Student Take-Home Paper
- PowerPoint Presentation

The Signs of Our Saviour | © 2009 Striving Together Publications

Suggested Classroom Schedule

Before Class	Complete attendance record. Provide students with coloring pages/activity pages.	
Opening	Welcome	
Prayer	Prayer requests and praise reports from the children	
Song Time		
Memory Verse	Matthew 4:19	
Song Time		
Object Lesson	Obedience	
Bible Lesson	Jesus Helps Peter Catch Fish	
Application/Invitation	Help saved students apply lesson. Invite unsaved students to receive Christ.	
Snack	Dirt Pudding Cups	
Review Game/ Questions	Matching	
Craft	Fishing Pole	
Closing	Announcements and Prayer Distribute take-home papers.	

Lesson Three Overview

Jesus Helps Peter Catch Fish

Theme—Jesus will bless us as we follow His instructions.

Scripture
Luke 5:1–11

Memory Verse
Matthew 4:19—*"And he saith unto them, Follow me, and I will make you fishers of men."*

Lesson Outline

Introducing the Story

The miracle we will study today occurred on the Sea of Galilee, in a boat belonging to Peter. We will learn that Jesus blesses obedience.

Telling the Story

1. **Jesus Teaching from a Boat** *(vv. 1–3)*

2. **Jesus Gives Peter Instructions** *(vv. 4–5)*

3. **Everyone Is Surprised by the Results** *(vv. 6–7, Ephesians 3:20)*

4. **Peter Is Humbled** *(vv. 8–9)*

5. **Jesus Has More Plans for Peter and His Friends** *(vv. 10–11, Acts 1:8)*

Applying the Story *(Matthew 4:19)*

As you obey Jesus, you can know He will bless you, as He blessed Peter with many fish. And as you follow Jesus, you can know He will use you just as He used Peter to catch men.

3 Lesson Three

Jesus Helps Peter Catch Fish

Theme: Jesus will bless us as we follow His instructions.

 ## Scripture

Luke 5:1–11

1 And it came to pass, that, as the people pressed upon him to hear the word of God, he stood by the lake of Gennesaret,
2 And saw two ships standing by the lake: but the fishermen were gone out of them, and were washing their nets.
3 And he entered into one of the ships, which was Simon's, and prayed him that he would thrust out a little from the land. And he sat down, and taught the people out of the ship.
4 Now when he had left speaking, he said unto Simon, Launch out into the deep, and let down your nets for a draught.
5 And Simon answering said unto him, Master, we have toiled all the night, and have taken nothing: nevertheless at thy word I will let down the net.
6 And when they had this done, they inclosed a great multitude of fishes: and their net brake.
7 And they beckoned unto their partners, which were in the other ship, that they should come and help them. And they came, and filled both the ships, so that they began to sink.
8 When Simon Peter saw it, he fell down at Jesus' knees, saying, Depart from me; for I am a sinful man, O Lord.
9 For he was astonished, and all that were with him, at the draught of the fishes which they had taken:
10 And so was also James, and John, the sons of Zebedee, which were partners with Simon. And Jesus said unto Simon, Fear not; from henceforth thou shalt catch men.
11 And when they had brought their ships to land, they forsook all, and followed him.

Memory Verse

Matthew 4:19
"And he saith unto them, Follow me, and I will make you fishers of men."

Lesson Three—Jesus Helps Peter Catch Fish

 # Teacher's Checklist

- ❏ Read Luke 5:1–11 daily
- ❏ Study Lesson Three
- ❏ Gather props for lesson—fishing net and picture of fishing boat
- ❏ Prepare snack—dirt pudding with gummy worms
- ❏ Gather materials for object lesson—square napkin, pencil
- ❏ Print and cut matching fish cards for review game from the Ministry Resource CD
- ❏ Prepare memory verse visual from the Ministry Resource CD. Print, cut, and attach adhesive to the memory verse (Matthew 4:19).
- ❏ Print "memory verse token" (one per student) from the Ministry Resource CD.
- ❏ Purchase for craft—dowels, fishing line, and fishing bobber for each student
- ❏ Gather other materials for craft—crayons, scissors, glue, and clear tape
- ❏ Print both of the fish templates for craft from the Teacher's Resource CD
- ❏ Print and duplicate Coloring Pages or Activity Pages on the Ministry Resource CD (one per student)
- ❏ Print and duplicate Take-Home Paper on the Ministry Resource CD (one per student)

 Snack Suggestion

Dirt Pudding Cups
To illustrate bait that can be used in fishing, prepare chocolate pudding cups. Sprinkle chocolate cookie crumbs on top of the pudding, and add a gummy worm coming out of the dirt.

38 | The Signs of Our Saviour | © 2009 Striving Together Publications

Lesson Three—Jesus Helps Peter Catch Fish

Bible Lesson

Scripture: Luke 5:1–11

INTRODUCING THE STORY

Have you ever chosen to obey when at first you weren't sure how your obedience would turn out? (Ask for examples from the students and provide your own examples.) How did the situation ultimately turn out?

When we obey our parents, teachers, and especially our Lord, we can trust that God always knows best! Peter learned that important lesson during the story we're going to look at today.

The first miracle of Jesus, which we learned about two weeks ago, occurred in the village of Cana. This city was just over fifteen miles from the Sea of Galilee (to the west). It was there that Jesus turned water into wine. The second miracle occurred closer to the Sea of Galilee, in a city right on the shore called Capernaum. It was there that a nobleman's son was healed. The miracle we will study today occurred on the Sea of Galilee, sometimes called the Lake of Gennesaret, in a boat belonging to Peter.

THE STORY

1. Jesus Teaching from a Boat (vv. 1–3)

People were beginning to gather in large crowds to hear Jesus teach and preach. Often the crowds became so large that Jesus had to find some unique way to position Himself so that everyone could see and hear Him.

Jesus saw two ships, but He chose to enter the boat of a fisherman named Peter, in order to preach to the crowd. I wonder if Peter ever had someone teach from his boat before? Probably not!

Jesus asked Peter to row the boat away from the shore a short distance so that He could begin teaching. (Jesus knew the flat surface of the lake's water would act as a "sounding board," which would amplify His voice as He spoke toward the people on the shore. How did Jesus know this would work? Well, since He created the lake, formed the human ear, and designed the way sound waves would operate, He had a pretty good idea it would work!)

Teaching Tip

Come into class wearing a rain slicker and hat. Consider bringing in a fishing pole and tackle box, as well, to get the attention of your students.

Teaching Tip

Use a map of Palestine during the ministry of Christ (available free from a number of sources on the Internet) to show your students the relationship between Cana, Capernaum, and the Sea of Galilee.

Use an Object

Picture of Fishing Boat
Show a picture of a fishing boat used in Bible times. These small boats stayed close to the shore in shallow water.

Teacher's Note

The New Testament writers used a variety of terms to refer to the Sea of Galilee. In today's passage, Luke called this body of water the "Lake of Gennesaret."

The Signs of Our Saviour | © 2009 Striving Together Publications

2. Jesus Gives Peter Instructions (vv. 4–5)

We do not know exactly what Jesus taught about on that day. He probably used the Old Testament Scriptures, maybe reminding the people about His Father's love and plan for them and about their disobedience to His commands. After Jesus finished teaching the people, He gave instructions to Peter. He told him to go fishing—to launch out into the deeper part of the sea and to let down his nets to catch fish.

We know from verse 2 that Peter and his fellow fishermen had recently finished a time of fishing, because they were washing their nets. These fishermen did not use poles and lines. They used nets instead. (For older students: Large fishing operations on the oceans still use nets today, lowering them into the water and sweeping up as many fish as they can.) Peter and his friends were most likely removing the seaweed and debris that had collected on their nets. They were probably not planning to fish again until later that day or the next.

Peter (also called Simon) probably thought that he was a more experienced fisherman than Jesus. But he also knew there was something very special about Jesus and His authority, so he obeyed. Before following Jesus' instructions, Peter did remind Him that they had worked all night, the night before, and had caught nothing. Maybe he was hoping with that news, Jesus would take back His command, but He did not. So Peter said, "Nevertheless, at thy word, I will let down the net," and he and his friends let down one of their nets. By saying this, Peter meant, "I will obey You."

Use an Object

Fishing Net
Bring in a fishing net (can be found at a local party store) and use it as a prop throughout your lesson.

Teacher's Note

In verse 5, Peter used the word, "Master." This word refers to someone who has rule over everything.

3. Everyone Is Surprised by the Results (vv. 6–7)

Do you think they were expecting to catch many fish, after having been out all night (night time was a better part of the day to catch fish), and catching nothing? Probably not! But they caught so many fish that 1) their net broke, 2) they had to ask for help from a nearby boat, and 3) both boats almost sank!

Maybe Peter and his friends should have let down more than just one net (after all, Jesus did say "nets"). I'm sure they would have, if they had known how many fish Jesus had waiting for them. We should remember that God often has greater blessings in store for us than we imagine, if we will simply do what He says.

Ephesians 3:20

20 *Now unto him that is able to do exceeding abundantly above all that we ask or think, according to the power that worketh in us,*

Jesus wants to surprise you with the blessings He has in store for your life. He wants to bless you more than you can imagine. He wants to use you more than you would understand. But His ability to bless you begins with your decision to obey.

Would Peter and his friends have caught any fish, had they not let down at least one net? What if they had said to Jesus, "We know much more about fishing than You, so we're not going to fish again today"? They would have missed out on the blessing, not only of catching the fish, but also of realizing what a wonderful God Jesus really is.

4. Peter Is Humbled (vv. 8–9)

Peter immediately knew that this situation was more than just Jesus knowing about a secret fishing hole! This was a miracle! He realized that Jesus was God—that He possessed great authority, and that He was very much in charge of the boat, the nets, and the fish…and that He deserved to be in charge of Peter's life, as well.

Peter bowed before the Lord Jesus in worship and humility. I'm sure he was ashamed for ever questioning the instructions of Jesus to let down their nets. James and John, who were brothers and also fishermen, were with Peter that day. They were also amazed and humbled over what they had just seen.

5. Jesus Has More Plans for Peter and His Friends (vv. 10–11)

Now that Peter, James, and John had a glimpse of who He really was, Jesus was ready to let them know He had more plans for them. Just like catching the fish that day, the plans Jesus had for the lives of Peter, James, and John were far beyond what they could have expected. He planned for them to become fishers of *men*!

Although this was an unforgettable moment for these men, it was only to be the first in a lifetime of following Jesus. They were not simply going to return to fishing the next day and repeat this story to their children and friends, as most fishermen do. Jesus would ask them to leave their boats and their nets behind and begin a lifetime of following Him. Instead of focusing their daily attention on finding and catching fish, they were going to begin "catching men" for Him!

He was going to train them to be His representatives—men who would tell others about Him, so they too could believe. And after conquering the Cross and the grave, He would leave them and a few others with the responsibility of spreading His Good News to the entire world.

When Peter, James, and John brought their ships to land, they left the fishing and followed the Lord.

Acts 1:8

8   *But ye shall receive power, after that the Holy Ghost is come upon you: and ye shall be witnesses unto me both in Jerusalem, and in all Judaea, and in Samaria, and unto the uttermost part of the earth.*

Chapter two of the book of Acts explains that on one day Peter preached about Jesus, and three thousand people decided to believe on Him as their Saviour. What Jesus had planned for Peter was amazing! It was better than Peter could have imagined!

God has great plans for you, too. And those plans will involve, in some way, helping others to hear the Gospel. We do not live in the same cities that Peter, James, and John did, nor do we live during the same time in history. But the one thing our lives have in common with theirs, is that God wants to use us to fish for men!

APPLYING THE STORY

Are you convinced that Jesus always knows best? For a moment, Peter may have thought that he knew better than Jesus about fishing. But did he? Why are we sometimes slow to obey our parents, our teachers, or our Lord? Do we think we are smarter than they? Do we think we are smarter than the Lord?

At the beginning of the story, Peter had some pride. But at the end of the story, he was humble. He was humble because he realized how much more wise, powerful, and good Jesus was than he.

When you **obey** Jesus, you can know He will bless you, as He blessed Peter with many fish.

- We obey Jesus when we obey the authorities in our lives.
- We obey Jesus when we obey His Word.

Verse 11 of our story tells us "they forsook all, and followed Him." As Matthew wrote down this story, he explained what Jesus said to Peter and his friends:

Matthew 4:19

19   And he saith unto them, Follow me, and I will make you fishers of men.

As you **follow** Jesus, you can know He will use you, just like He used Peter to catch men.

- We follow Jesus when we do what He wants us to do when He wants us to do it.
- We follow Jesus when we tell others about Him.

Review Game/Questions

Matching
Materials Needed
- "Match Game" template on Ministry Resource CD
- Cardstock

Instructions
Print on cardstock. Print numbers on one side. Flip and print fish on the other side. Cut into fourths.

Place the squares (fish side down, numbers showing) in a pocket chart. (You can also line up the squares on the chalkboard rail or lay face down on a table if a pocket chart is not available). Divide the class into teams. Ask Team One a review question. Call on a student to answer. If the student answers correctly, that student calls out two numbers to be turned over. The teacher turns over the two squares and checks to see if the two fish match. If they do match, that team gets a point. Repeat for Team Two.

Object
The team with the most matches wins.

1. The Lake of Gennesaret was also known as what body of water?
   Answer: Sea of Galilee

Lesson Three—Jesus Helps Peter Catch Fish

2. How many ships did Jesus see?
    Answer: Two

3. Whose ship did Jesus enter?
    Answer: Simon Peter's

4. What did Jesus do first on Peter's boat?
    Answer: He taught the people.

5. After teaching the people, what did Jesus ask Peter to do?
    Answer: Launch out into the deep and let down your nets.

6. What was Peter's response to Jesus' command?
    Answer: We already did that and caught nothing!

7. Did Peter obey Jesus?
    Answer: Yes

8. When Peter obeyed and let down his net, what happened?
    Answer: He caught fish.

9. After catching so many fish, what did Peter do?
    Answer: He called on the other ship to help him.

10. Because there were so many fish, what happened?
    Answer: The boats began to sink.

11. Why do you think Peter fell down at Jesus' knees?
    Answer: Peter just witnessed a miracle. Knowing that Jesus was God, Peter felt unworthy.

12. Jesus told Peter, James, and John that they would now catch a different kind of fish. What did Jesus want them to "catch" now?
    Answer: Men

13. What does it mean to "catch men"?
    Answer: Tell others about Jesus, so they too can trust Him as their Saviour.

14. When they brought their ships to land, what did Peter, James and John do?
    Answer: Forsook all and followed Jesus.

Lesson Three—Jesus Helps Peter Catch Fish

Teaching the Memory Verse

Matthew 4:19

19 And he saith unto them, Follow me, and I will make you fishers of men.

1. Print visual aids on cardstock and cut out for Matthew 4:19.

2. Attach a magnet to the back of each visual. (If you do not have a magnetic board, then you can substitute velcro tabs for magnets and use on a flannel board).

3. Place visuals on board.

4. Have your students turn to Matthew 4:19. Read Matthew 4:19 together.

    Ask them if any of the words of this verse are in red. Then explain, "What does that mean? Jesus spoke these words!"

    Jesus wants us to "follow Him." We should imitate Christ in our lives.

    Jesus wants to make us fishers of men—telling others the Gospel of Jesus Christ.

5. Have the students repeat the verse several times, each time imitating a different way of saying the verse. (Marching in place while saying the verse, clapping your hands over your head, standing on one foot, patting head and rubbing tummy, hopping on one foot)

Use companion flashcards found in Visual Resource Packet or images found on Ministry Resource CD.

Resource CD

There is a memory verse token on the Ministry Resource CD that may be given to each child. Print on white paper.

Lesson Three—Jesus Helps Peter Catch Fish

Object Lesson—Obedience

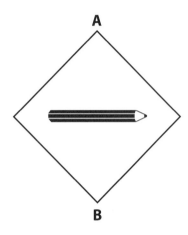

Materials needed:
- Square napkin (cloth or paper)
- Pencil

For the teacher:

Place the napkin in a diamond shape on a flat surface. Lay the pencil across the center of the napkin. Fold "Tip B" up and over "Tip A," over lapping it about ¼ inch. The pencil should be covered.

Keeping the pencil in place, tightly roll the napkin from the fold (bottom to the top). Continue rolling until the first corner flips over. (This is very important, because if you were to keep rolling the napkin until the second corner flips over, the pencil would remain inside the napkin.)

Unroll the napkin, and you should see that the pencil is now on the top (appearing to have penetrated the napkin from inside to outside).

To the class:

God promises us that when we obey, we will be successful or blessed (Jeremiah 7:23; Deuteronomy 6:3). I need a helper. If my helper obeys me, he/she will be able to pass this pencil from the inside of the napkin to the outside.

Roll the pencil in the napkin until the first corner flips. Say to your helper, "Tap the pencil with your finger three times. Now let's unroll it, and look! The pencil is now outside on top of the napkin.

"Let's try this again, but I want you to disobey. Instead of tapping three times tap the pencil four times." Again, roll the pencil up until the second corner flips. Have the volunteer tap four times on the pencil. Unroll and the pencil will still be inside the napkin.

Let this be a reminder that when we obey we will be successful. Let's obey every command of God!

46 | The Signs of Our Saviour | © 2009 Striving Together Publications

Lesson Three—Jesus Helps Peter Catch Fish

Craft—Fishing Pole

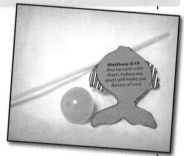

Getting It Together

Per student:
1 12 inch wood dowel
1 18 inch piece of fishing line
1 fishing bobber
1 template of the fish from the resource CD
1 template of the fish with the verse from the resource CD
Tape
Crayons
Glue

Putting It Together

1. Print and cut out the two templates of the fish.
2. Color the fish.
3. Glue the two fish together, back to back, leaving the mouth of the fish unglued.
4. Tie the fishing line to the top of the wooden craft dowel, securing it with tape.
5. String the fishing bobber to the fishing line.
6. Place the bottom of the fishing line into the fish's mouth, gluing the mouth shut with the fishing line inside.

Seeing It Together

Let's remember to be a follower of Jesus by fishing for men! Who will you tell about Christ this week?

Additional Resources

Find the following items on the Ministry Resource CD:
- Coloring Page (for younger children)
- Activity Page (for older children)
- Student Take-Home Paper
- PowerPoint Presentation

The Signs of Our Saviour | © 2009 Striving Together Publications

Suggested Classroom Schedule

Before Class		Complete attendance record. Provide students with coloring pages/activity pages.
Opening		Welcome
Prayer		Prayer requests and praise reports from the children
Song Time		
Memory Verses		John 1:41–42a
Song Time		
Object Lesson		Each One Bring One
Bible Lesson		Jesus Heals a Friend
Application/Invitation		Help saved students apply lesson. Invite unsaved students to receive Christ.
Snack		Fruit Roll Ups
Review Game/ Questions		Help, I'm Stuck!
Craft		Cross Bag
Closing		Announcements and Prayer Distribute take home-papers.

Lesson Four Overview

Jesus Heals a Friend
Theme—We can help to bring our friends to Jesus.

Scripture
Mark 2:1–12

Memory Verses
John 1:41–42a—"He first findeth his own brother Simon, and saith unto him, We have found the Messias, which is, being interpreted, the Christ. And he brought him to Jesus...."

Lesson Outline

Introducing the Story
The men in today's story climbed on the roof of a house! Their friend needed help getting to where Jesus was, and they realized they could help him get there.

Telling the Story
1. **A Crowded House Where Jesus Was Preaching** (vv. 1–2, 1 Corinthians 1:21, Titus 1:3)

2. **Four Men and Their Sick Friend** (v. 3, Psalm 142:4, John 5:7)

3. **A Strange Way to Enter a House!** (v. 4, James 2:18)
   —Flash Card 4.1

4. **Jesus Forgives Sins** (vv. 5–10, Romans 5:12, 3:28)
   —Flash Card 4.2

5. **Jesus Heals the Friend** (vv. 11–12, Psalm 94:11)
   —Flash Card 4.3

Applying the Story
We learn from the four men in this story that a real friend will help others get to Jesus. Is there someone who needs your help getting to Jesus?

4 Lesson Four

Jesus Heals a Friend

Theme: We can help to bring our friends to Jesus.

Scripture

Mark 2:1–12

1 And again he entered into Capernaum after some days; and it was noised that he was in the house.
2 And straightway many were gathered together, insomuch that there was no room to receive them, no, not so much as about the door: and he preached the word unto them.
3 And they come unto him, bringing one sick of the palsy, which was borne of four.
4 And when they could not come nigh unto him for the press, they uncovered the roof where he was: and when they had broken it up, they let down the bed wherein the sick of the palsy lay.
5 When Jesus saw their faith, he said unto the sick of the palsy, Son, thy sins be forgiven thee.
6 But there were certain of the scribes sitting there, and reasoning in their hearts,
7 Why doth this man thus speak blasphemies? who can forgive sins but God only?
8 And immediately when Jesus perceived in his spirit that they so reasoned within themselves, he said unto them, Why reason ye these things in your hearts?
9 Whether is it easier to say to the sick of the palsy, Thy sins be forgiven thee; or to say, Arise, and take up thy bed, and walk?
10 But that ye may know that the Son of man hath power on earth to forgive sins, (he saith to the sick of the palsy,)
11 I say unto thee, Arise, and take up thy bed, and go thy way into thine house.
12 And immediately he arose, took up the bed, and went forth before them all; insomuch that they were all amazed, and glorified God, saying, We never saw it on this fashion.

Memory Verses

John 1:41–42a
"He first findeth his own brother Simon, and saith unto him, We have found the Messias, which is, being interpreted, the Christ. And he brought him to Jesus…"

Lesson Four—Jesus Heals a Friend

 Teacher's Checklist

 Snack Suggestion

Cut "Fruit Roll Ups" into long rectangles and roll back up. Tie with licorice rope. Use the snack to represent the bed the lame man carried away after he had been healed.

- ❑ Read Mark 2:1–12 daily
- ❑ Study Lesson Four
- ❑ Flashcards 4.1–4.3
- ❑ Prepare snack—Fruit Roll Ups and pull-apart licorice ropes
- ❑ Gather for object lesson—128 pieces of candy, a bag, and a clear bowl
- ❑ Memory verse flashcards for John 1:41–42a.
- ❑ Purchase for craft—ribbon, construction paper, and white lunch bags
- ❑ Gather for craft—hole punch, crayons, and scissors
- ❑ Print Cross template for the craft from the Ministry Resource CD
- ❑ Print invitation card templates for the craft from the Ministry Resource CD
- ❑ Print and duplicate Coloring Pages or Activity Pages on the Ministry Resource CD (one per student)
- ❑ Print and duplicate Take-Home Paper on the Ministry Resource CD (one per student)

50 | The Signs of Our Saviour | © 2009 Striving Together Publications

Lesson Four—Jesus Heals a Friend

Bible Lesson

Scripture: Mark 2:1–12

INTRODUCING THE STORY

Have you ever seen someone working on the roof of a house? As a child, you should never try to go up on top of a roof, because it can be very dangerous. But sometimes men who have certain jobs must work on roofs. Can you think of jobs like this? Examples would include a carpenter, a roofer, and a chimney sweep.

The men in today's story went on top of the roof of a house for a very different reason! Their reason for being on the roof of a house was that they were helping their friend. No, their friend was not a roofer or a chimney-sweep! Their friend needed help getting to where Jesus was. And they realized they could help him get there.

THE STORY

1. A Crowded House Where Jesus Was Preaching (vv. 1–2)

You know by now that in His ministry, Jesus turned water into wine at a wedding in Cana. He healed a nobleman's son in Capernaum. He caught fish with Peter, and called him and others to follow Him in catching men. He also preached in many different cities, and He healed others who were sick.

And in the story we read today, we see him back in Capernaum. He is in that city, inside someone's house. And the house is jam-packed with people. I wonder if it were the nobleman's house? I'm sure He would've been welcomed there! Whoever's house it was, there were people everywhere. People were probably sitting on the furniture, standing on the stairway, peering around corners, and even looking in through open windows and doors.

Why had these people filled this person's house? Because Jesus was there… and because He was preaching! Wouldn't you have loved to hear Jesus preach in person? Jesus had such a wonderful testimony, and His preaching was so powerful and interesting, that people gathered in large numbers to hear Him.

Don't ever forget how important preaching is! The Bible tells us that God has chosen preaching as one of His special tools in helping people hear about Him.

1 Corinthians 1:21

21 For after that in the wisdom of God the world by wisdom
knew not God, it pleased God by the foolishness of
preaching to save them that believe.

Titus 1:3

3 But hath in due times manifested his word through
preaching, which is committed unto me according to the
commandment of God our Saviour;

2. Four Men and Their Sick Friend (v. 3)

To this crowded house came four men carrying their very sick friend on a bed. "Sick of the palsy" means that the man's legs were paralyzed—he could not move them, and he could not walk. I am sure this man was thankful that he had friends willing to help him.

Are you the kind of friend who will help someone in his time of need? Even more importantly, are you the kind of friend who will help someone get to Jesus Christ? You cannot save someone's soul any more than these four men could heal their friend. But you can do what they did—help bring your friends to Jesus, so they may meet Him!

One of the writers of an Old Testament psalm (one of the songs sung by the Jewish people), explained how sad it is to not find anyone who cares for you.

Psalm 142:4

4 I looked on my right hand, and beheld, but there was no
man that would know me: refuge failed me; no man cared
for my soul.

During Jesus' ministry, He met a man who—unlike the man with palsy in this story—had no one to help him while in his condition.

John 5:7

7 The impotent man answered him, Sir, I have no man, when
the water is troubled, to put me into the pool: but while I
am coming, another steppeth down before me.

3. A Strange Way to Enter a House! (v. 4)

When these men arrived at the house with their friend and saw the crowd, they discovered that it was going to be even more difficult to get their friend to Jesus than they thought. After trying to use the door, the men realized they needed a different plan.

Many houses in Galilee were constructed with flat roofs, which contained "porches" where people would sit when they wanted to relax outside. Because of this, there were usually ladders or steps, which led to the roofs. But that fact does not make the story any easier! They still had to find a way inside.

Flash Card 4.1

From the roof, the men found an area where they could remove some of the roof tiles (like shingles, but made of clay). Verse 4 tells us they actually had to break the tiles apart. I wonder what the owner of the house thought? With the crowd, he may not have even been able to see exactly what was happening!

They carefully lowered the man on the mat into the room near Jesus. The Bible tells us that Jesus "saw their faith." This reminds us that our relationship with Jesus needs to become more than just decisions we have made in our hearts, but these decisions must be worked out in our lives to be seen of others.

> **James 2:18**
> 18 Yea, a man may say, Thou hast faith, and I have works: shew me thy faith without thy works, and I will shew thee my faith by my works.

4. Jesus Forgives Sins (vv. 5–10)

Now, you may think that the greatest need in this man's life was the healing of his paralyzed legs. And that was his greatest physical need. But Jesus is always first concerned with our spiritual needs. What was this man's greatest spiritual need? It was the same as the greatest spiritual need in people's lives today—the forgiveness of our sins. Our sin separates us from God, from a home in Heaven, and from every other good thing He wants to share with us. Those things can only become ours if our sin is forgiven and removed.

Lesson Four—Jesus Heals a Friend

Romans 5:12

12 *Wherefore, as by one man sin entered into the world, and death by sin; and so death passed upon all men, for that all have sinned:*

Flash Card 4.2

So the first thing that happened to this man is that Jesus looked at him and said, "Son, thy sins be forgiven thee."

Why was Jesus able to forgive this man's sins? Jesus' forgiveness was in response to his faith. The man's desire to be brought to Jesus demonstrated his faith in God's Son.

Romans 3:28

28 *Therefore we conclude that a man is justified by faith without the deeds of the law.*

This paralyzed man did not need to do one single thing in order to be forgiven of his sins. He simply needed—like his friends—to put his faith in Jesus. What could he do from his bed, suffering from palsy? He could not do many things others could do. (Give examples: He couldn't easily be baptized. He couldn't work a job to earn a salary. He couldn't walk to church.) But, he could receive the forgiveness because of his faith in Christ.

5. Jesus Heals the Friend (vv. 11–12)

Among the crowd in the house were a number of Pharisees. Jesus knew what they were thinking (verse 8). They were thinking, "This man cannot forgive sins. Only God can do that!"

Did you know that Jesus knows exactly what you are thinking at all times?

Teacher's Note

The Pharisees "reasoned" a great truth in their second question, "Who can forgive sins but God only?"

Psalm 94:11

11 *The LORD knoweth the thoughts of man, that they are vanity.*

Jesus answered their doubt-filled question with a question of His own. He asked whether it's easier to tell someone their sins are forgiven, or to tell a paralyzed man to rise up and walk. If Jesus tells someone that their sins

54 The Signs of Our Saviour | © 2009 Striving Together Publications

are forgiven, you cannot tell from the outside whether the act has actually taken place. However, if He tells a man with palsy to rise up and walk, and the man does, then no one could possibly question his power and authority as God's Son.

So Jesus said to the man, "Arise, and take up thy bed, and go thy way…" (verse 11). And he did! Everyone in the house was amazed. And everyone agreed that they had never seen anything like that happen before.

Flash Card 4.3

APPLYING THE STORY

We learn from the four men in this story, that a real friend will help others get to Jesus. Is there someone who needs your help getting to Jesus? Maybe a neighbor on your street, or a friend in your school, or a grandparent, or a cousin, or even one of your parents needs your help in getting to Jesus.

What are some things you can do to help those people get to Jesus?
- Give them a tract.
- Invite them to church with you.
- Write them a letter and explain God's love for them.
- Ask them if you can tell them what you've learned from the Bible.

Lesson Four—Jesus Heals a Friend

 **Review Game/Questions**

Help, I'm Stuck!
Materials Needed
None

Instructions
Divide the class into two teams. Choose one person to come up to the front of the class from each team. Have the two students stand against the wall, as if they were stuck. Begin asking questions, alternating between teams. When a student answers correctly, he may go to his teammate that is stuck on the wall and release one body part (his head, left arm, right arm, left leg, and then right leg).

Object
The first team to release the teammate wins.

1. Today's lesson took place in what city?
   Answer: Capernaum

2. What was Jesus doing in the house?
   Answer: Preaching

3. Friends brought a man who was sick to see Jesus. What sickness did he have?
   Answer: Sick of Palsy

4. How many friends brought him to see Jesus?
   Answer: Four

5. Why do you think the men wanted their friend to see Jesus?
   Answer: They knew Jesus could help him.

6. What did the men do when they could not get into the house because there were so many people?
   Answer: They uncovered the roof and lowered their friend inside.

7. How did Jesus heal the man?
   Answer: He spoke the words, "Son, thy sins be forgiven thee."

8. Not everyone was happy with what Jesus had said. Who was unhappy?
   Answer: The Scribes

9. How did Jesus know what they were thinking?
   Answer: He is God, and He knows what everyone is thinking.

10. What are some ways we can invite others to church?
    Answer: Give them a tract, write them a letter, etc.

Teaching the Memory Verse

John 1:41–42a

41 He first findeth his own brother Simon, and saith unto him, We have found the Messias, which is, being interpreted, the Christ.

42 And he brought him to Jesus….

Cut out visuals for John 1:41–42a. (On Ministry Resource CD)

Do your friends know Jesus? If you truly love or care for your friends, don't just enjoy their company now. Make sure your friends know the way to Heaven so that you can spend eternity together. Tell your friends about Jesus today. (Read John 1:41–42a)

Choose five students to help hold the posters. Repeat the verse several times. When the class has a good grasp of the verse, ask one of the helping students to turn around with his poster so the words are now hidden to the class. Have the class say the verse again. Repeat until all students holding a poster are facing the wall and the class can say the verse without any help.

Use companion flashcards found in Visual Resource Packet or images found on Ministry Resource CD.

Lesson Four—Jesus Heals a Friend

Object Lesson—Each One Bring One

Materials:
- 128 pieces of candy
- Brown lunch bag
- Clear glass bowl—just large enough to hold the candy

Lesson:

At home, place candy in brown lunch bag. In class, set the bowl on the table. Tell the students this bowl represents our Sunday school class.

Take one piece of the candy from the bag. This piece of candy represents a Christian. Tell the class, "This candy could represent you!"

This Christian went home from Sunday school and told his friend about Jesus and invited him to Sunday school. The next Sunday there were two children in Sunday school (place another piece of candy into the bowl).

Now two children went home from Sunday school and each told a friend about Jesus and invited them to Sunday school. The next Sunday there were four children in Sunday school (place two more pieces of candy into the bowl).

Repeat:
- 4 children bring 4 children (add 4 more pieces of candy) = 8 pieces
- 8 children bring 8 children (add 8 more pieces of candy) =16 pieces
- 16 children bring 16 children (add 16 more pieces of candy) = 32 pieces
- 32 children bring 32 children (add 32 more pieces of candy) = 64 pieces
- 64 children bring 64 children (add the rest of the candy) = 128 pieces

Wow! Look what can happen when we will consistently invite others to hear about Jesus! In just 8 weeks, the Sunday school class grew from 1 person to 128 people!

Give each student two pieces of the candy. One for them and one to share. Remind them that as they share their candy, to share the most important truth of all, that Jesus loves them and died for them. And, remember to invite them to Sunday school.

(You may also relate this object lesson to salvation and say this bowl represents Heaven and the candy represents a soulwinner.)

Lesson Four—Jesus Heals a Friend

Craft—Cross Bag

Getting It Together

Ribbon
Cardstock, various colors
Single hole punch
Crayons
Scissors

Per student:
1   White sack lunch bag
1   Cross verse template located on the resource CD
2   Invitation card template located on the resource CD

Putting It Together

1. Start by printing and cutting out the Cross template on white paper.
2. Color the Cross template.
3. Print and cut out 2 sets of the invitation cards (per student) on colored cardstock.
4. Cut 6 inches of the sack lunch bag off of the top. (Optional: Cut the top of each bag with craft designed scissors.)
5. Glue the colored Cross template to one side of the bag.
6. Place the invitation cards in to the bag.
7. Hole punch 2 holes to the top of the bag.
8. Tie the top of the bag with any color ribbon.

Seeing It Together

We want to bring our friends to Jesus. These cards will help us in telling our friends about Jesus.

Additional Resources

Find the following items on the Ministry Resource CD:

- Coloring Page (for younger children)
- Activity Page (for older children)
- Student Take-Home Paper
- PowerPoint Presentation

Suggested Classroom Schedule

Before Class	Complete attendance record. Provide students with coloring pages/activity pages.
Opening	Welcome
Prayer	Prayer requests and praise reports from the children
Song Time	
Memory Verse	Matthew 28:18
Song Time	
Object Lesson	No Power
Bible Lesson	Jesus Raises the Widow's Son
Application/Invitation	Help saved students apply lesson. Invite unsaved students to receive Christ.
Snack	Cookies and Powerade
Review Game/ Questions	Pick-a-Dot
Craft	Widow's Son
Closing	Announcements and Prayer Distribute take home-papers.

Lesson Five Overview

Jesus Raises the Widow's Son

Theme—Jesus has authority over death and life.

Scripture
Luke 7:11-17

Memory Verse
Matthew 28:18 — "And Jesus came and spake unto them, saying, All power is given unto me in heaven and in earth."

Lesson Outline

Introducing the Story
In the story today, a man died. We find out that his mother was very sad, just as one of us would be. But when Jesus came to her city, things changed for her very quickly!

Telling the Story
1. **A Funeral in Nain** (vv. 11–12)

2. **Jesus Shows Compassion** (v. 13, Matthew 9:36a, Psalm 86:15)

3. **The Son Rises Up and Speaks** (vv. 14–15, John 11:25)

4. **People Praise Jesus and His Father** (vv. 16–17, 1 Samuel 12:24, Psalm 30:12)

Applying the Story (Ephesians 2:1)
Jesus showed His power over death in the city of Nain. But Jesus has authority not only over physical death, but also spiritual death. If you have asked Jesus Christ to be your Saviour, He has brought you back to spiritual life. The miracle that happened in Nain has already happened in your life.

5 Lesson Five

Jesus Raises the Widow's Son

Theme: Jesus has authority over death and life.

Scripture

Luke 7:11–17

11 And it came to pass the day after, that he went into a city called Nain; and many of his disciples went with him, and much people.

12 Now when he came nigh to the gate of the city, behold, there was a dead man carried out, the only son of his mother, and she was a widow: and much people of the city was with her.

13 And when the Lord saw her, he had compassion on her, and said unto her, Weep not.

14 And he came and touched the bier: and they that bare him stood still. And he said, Young man, I say unto thee, Arise.

15 And he that was dead sat up, and began to speak. And he delivered him to his mother.

16 And there came a fear on all: and they glorified God, saying, That a great prophet is risen up among us; and, That God hath visited his people.

17 And this rumour of him went forth throughout all Judaea, and throughout all the region round about.

Memory Verse

Matthew 28:18

"And Jesus came and spake unto them, saying, All power is given unto me in heaven and in earth."

Lesson Five—Jesus Raises the Widow's Son

Teacher's Checklist

- ❑ Read Luke 7:11–17 daily
- ❑ Study Lesson Five
- ❑ For lesson—dry erase marker or chalk
- ❑ Prepare snack—Powerade and cookies
- ❑ Object lesson—various electrical gadgets
- ❑ Print and cut out "Pick-a-Dot" review game from the Ministry Resource CD
- ❑ Purchase for craft—Styrofoam cups, Band-Aids, wiggle eyes, and yarn
- ❑ Gather for craft—glue, markers, and scissors
- ❑ Print verse template for craft from the Ministry Resource CD
- ❑ Print and duplicate Coloring Pages or Activity Pages on the Ministry Resource CD (one per student)
- ❑ Print and duplicate Take-Home Paper on the Ministry Resource CD (one per student)

Serve cookies and *Powerade* to reinforce the truth that God has all power and authority in our lives!

Lesson Five—Jesus Raises the Widow's Son

Bible Lesson

Scripture: Luke 7:11–17

INTRODUCING THE STORY

Can you remember a time when you were very sad or disappointed? Something probably happens every week that disappoints us in some way. Some are small disappointments, such as receiving a poor grade on a test. Maybe we broke our favorite toy or ripped our favorite shirt. Or, maybe we were disappointed when our mom served a meal that we did not exactly like.

However, some things that happen to us are huge disappointments, and they cause great sadness. You may find out that someone you know and love has died, and you will not see them again. Some of you know exactly how terrible that feels because you have experienced it. Some of you have not experienced that, but will someday. Here on earth, the greatest sadness anyone can experience usually happens when someone we love dies.

In the story we will read today, a man has died. In this story, we find out that his mother was very sad, just as one of us would be. But when Jesus came to her city, things changed very quickly! Would you like to find out how this very sad woman became a very happy woman after spending just a few minutes with Jesus? Let's back up, and I'll tell you how it happened.

Draw It!

THE STORY

1. A Funeral in Nain (vv. 11–12)

As Jesus traveled from city to city, preaching, teaching, and performing miracles, He came, according to Luke chapter 7, to the city of Nain. This city was about fifteen miles southwest of the Sea of Galilee, where Jesus had helped Peter catch the great number of fish. This was the only time we know that Jesus went to this particular city. This was also one of the first times Jesus traveled with His disciples and a large group. He was beginning to teach and train these men about how to serve Him with their lives.

Nain was a city surrounded by walls. Many cities had walls around them in those days, to keep enemy armies out. These cities had gates, which

Teaching Tip

Nain—pronounced NAY-in.

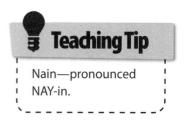

Draw It!

The Signs of Our Saviour | © 2009 Striving Together Publications

Lesson Five—Jesus Raises the Widow's Son

Draw It!

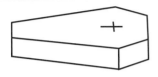

would open and close. This is where most people would come in and go out of the city.

As Jesus and His disciples came near the gate of the city, they saw a large group of people walking together. They were preparing to leave the city through the gate. This group of people, coming in the direction of Jesus, appeared to be very sad. Then Jesus saw that they were carrying the body of a man who had recently died.

This man's mother was there, with tears of sadness running down her face. Her husband had died sometime before this, making her a widow. Now, to make matters even worse, her only son had died, leaving her all alone.

Teacher's Note

Compassion: Sympathetic pity and concern for the sufferings or misfortunes of others with an urge to help

2. Jesus Shows Compassion (v. 13)

When Jesus saw her, He felt compassion. Often, when Jesus saw someone with a need, He allowed what He saw with His eyes to affect His heart and produce compassion.

> **Matthew 9:36a**
>
> *36a But when he saw the multitudes, he was moved with compassion on them…*

Someone once said, "Compassion is your hurt in my heart."

Sometimes we see people who have needs, and we do not stop and allow their pain to cause compassion in our hearts. We might think, "That's their problem. Why should I worry about it?" But this is not how Jesus felt about people. When Jesus saw people who had needs, He felt compassion toward them, and He showed love to them.

One of the wonderful characteristics of our Heavenly Father is that He is "full of compassion."

Draw It!

> **Psalm 86:15**
>
> *15 But thou, O Lord, art a God full of compassion, and gracious, longsuffering, and plenteous in mercy and truth.*

Jesus encouraged the woman, telling her to "weep not." Then, He came to where the men were carrying the body.

64 | The Signs of Our Saviour | © 2009 Striving Together Publications

3. The Son Rises Up and Speaks (vv. 14–15)

Jesus touched the bier the men were carrying, on which the dead man's body laid. (A "bier" was a flat bed or piece of lumber on which bodies were carried, in preparation for being buried.) The men stopped when Jesus touched the bier.

Jesus spoke to the man: "Young man, I say unto thee, Arise." Immediately, the young man sat up from the bed and began speaking!

This was the first time Jesus raised someone from the dead. Later in His ministry, He raised others, and then He would rise from the dead Himself. Isn't it wonderful to know that Jesus Christ, our Saviour, has all power—even power over death! Some time after this, Jesus spoke to a lady named Martha, whose brother had died. See what He told Martha about His power over death:

John 11:25

25 Jesus said unto her, I am the resurrection, and the life: he that believeth in me, though he were dead, yet shall he live:

4. People Praise Jesus and His Father (vv. 16–17)

At first, the people were fearful over what had happened. Jesus showed, in that moment, exactly how powerful He was.

Fearing the Lord does not mean that we are scared of Him. Fearing God means that we realize His greatness. When we fear God, we recognize that we are accountable to Him and we understand He could judge and punish us forever, based on our sin.

1 Samuel 12:24

24 Only fear the LORD, and serve him in truth with all your heart: for consider how great things he hath done for you.

When we are saved and consider that He has forgiven us, this fear turns into love and joy. Instead of punishing us, as we deserve, He is going to give us a wonderful home in Heaven to enjoy Him.

The people standing by quickly realized that though Jesus had all power and authority, He was also kind, compassionate, and good. And so

Draw It!

they glorified God. They said to one another that God had visited His people, because only God could raise the dead! They must have said how wonderful it was that God would send such a man to bring this widow such joy, by giving her son back to her.

The people who saw this miracle went home and told their families. Then they went to work the next day and told the people with whom they worked. As their children went to school, they told their friends about the miracle. Families told their friends and relatives from different towns about this amazing miracle that occurred. Before long, many people in many cities had heard about Jesus and His great power. All throughout Judaea, they heard what Jesus had done.

This is still how people today should hear about Jesus. When Jesus does things for us, we should tell others. This is how we glorify God—by speaking to others about what He has done for us. We should not be silent about His goodness.

Psalm 30:12

12 To the end that my glory may sing praise to thee, and not be silent. O LORD my God, I will give thanks unto thee for ever.

Draw It!

APPLYING THE STORY

Jesus showed His power over death in the city of Nain. But Jesus has authority over not only physical death but also spiritual death.

The Bible explains that without God, we are like that dead man. We need Jesus to come and give us life. Sure, our bodies are alive. But spiritually we are dead, and like the dead man in Nain, we are being carried off to a future separated from God. This is why being saved is called being "born again" (John 3:3, 7; 1 Peter 1:23). When we ask Jesus Christ to be our Saviour and to forgive our sin, we are made alive, as the man being carried on the bed in Luke chapter 7.

The Bible word for being brought back to life, as this man in Nain, is "quickened."

Ephesians 2:1

1 And you hath he quickened, who were dead in trespasses and sins;

Lesson Five—Jesus Raises the Widow's Son

If you have asked Jesus Christ to be your Saviour, He has given you spiritual life. The miracle that happened in Nain has already happened in your heart.

If you have not yet asked Jesus Christ to be your Saviour, you may choose to do so today! If you believe that Jesus is who He said He was, God's Son, and if you realize you need Him as your Saviour, the next step is to ask Him to save you and to forgive your sin. You may talk with one of the teachers today and have your questions answered about making this important decision!

Review Game/Questions

Pick-a-Dot

Materials Needed
- Cardstock
- Visual Template from Ministry Resource CD

Instructions
Print on different colors of cardstock and cut out the visual for Pick a Dot. Arrange on board. (Use a pocket chart, Velcro dots, magnets or tape to adhere to board.) Divide the class into teams. Alternate asking questions between the teams. When a student answers a question correctly, have him/her go to the board and pick a dot. Remove the dot from the board and look on the back side to see how many points that team receives.

Object
The team with the highest point total wins!

1. What is the name of the city in today's lesson?
   Answer: Nain

2. Who was traveling with Jesus?
   Answer: Many of His disciples and a lot of people

3. As they entered the gate, what did they see?
   Answer: A dead man being carried out of the city.

Lesson Five—Jesus Raises the Widow's Son

4. What do we know about the man's mother?
    Answer: She was a widow, and he was her only son.

5. Was the widow alone?
    Answer: No, many people from the city were with her.

6. When Jesus saw her, the Bible said He had compassion on her. What did He say to her?
    Answer: Weep not.

7. What did Jesus tell her son?
    Answer: Arise.

8. How did the people respond after the miracle?
    Answer: They were in awe and glorified God.

9. Why do you think the people said, "That God hath visited his people"?
    Answer: There was no mistaking, Jesus raised the dead. Only God can do that.

10. What happened throughout Judaea and the surrounding regions?
    Answer: They heard what Jesus did.

Lesson Five—Jesus Raises the Widow's Son

 # Teaching the Memory Verse

Matthew 28:18

18   And Jesus came and spake unto them, saying, All power is given unto me in heaven and in earth.

We have all been around some powerful people and some powerful objects. Ask students to name something or someone powerful. Even though those things are powerful, they do not compare to the power of God. He is all-powerful! God is the only One with power to raise the dead, as we learned in today's lesson. Not only does Jesus have authority over physical death, He also has power over spiritual death. Only Jesus can save us from our sin and give us eternal life in Heaven.

Open your Bible and read Matthew 28:18. Place flash cards on chalkboard tray. This week we will teach the student to use sign language to remember the verse. They will be able to share this verse to someone who knows sign language.

Use companion flash cards found in Visual Resource Packet or images found on Ministry Resource CD. Also, refer to the Ministry Resource CD for the video containing the sign language for this verse.

Lesson Five—Jesus Raises the Widow's Son

 # Object Lesson—No Power

Materials Needed:
Electrical gadgets (such as an electric screw driver, blender, electric toothbrush, fan) (You can use one to illustrate or several.)

Demonstration:
Begin to use your electrical tool in a manual fashion. (For instance, attempt to brush your teeth with your electric toothbrush on "off." Stir a drink in the blender using a spoon. Fan yourself with your hand while standing in front of the fan. Use the electric screwdriver like you were using a regular screwdriver.)

Hopefully, one of the student will notice that none of these are plugged in or turned on. These tools were designed to work under power.

Application:
In the same way, we are designed to work under God's power. We will be most effective when we do what God wants us to do under His Power!

 # Additional Resources

Find the following items on the Ministry Resource CD:
- Coloring Page (for younger children)
- Activity Page (for older children)
- Student Take-Home Paper
- PowerPoint Presentation

Lesson Five—Jesus Raises the Widow's Son

Craft—Widow's Son

Getting It Together

Yarn (hair color)
Glue- fast drying glue
Markers
Scissors

Per student:
1 foam cup
1 Band-Aid
2 Wiggly craft eyes
1 Verse template located on the Ministry Resource CD

Putting It Together

1. Print and cut out the verse template.
2. Place the foam cup upside down.
3. Glue the verse template around the bottom rim of the cup. (When gluing items to a foam cup, we recommend using a fast drying glue.)
4. Cut out small pieces of yarn for the hair.
5. Glue the hair to the top of the cup.
6. Glue the eyes to the middle of the cup to make the face.
7. Have the students color and decorate the cup to look like a person.
8. Place the Band-Aid on his face to represent that he was sick.

Seeing It Together

Jesus has the authority over life and death. There is no problem too big for the Lord! He can help us in every situation.

The Signs of Our Saviour | © 2009 Striving Together Publications

Suggested Classroom Schedule

Before Class	Complete attendance record. Provide students with coloring pages/activity pages.
Opening	Welcome
Prayer	Prayer requests and praise reports from the children
Song Time	
Memory Verse	Psalm 46:1
Song Time	
Object Lesson	God's Protection
Bible Lesson	Jesus Calms the Storm
Application/Invitation	Help saved students apply lesson. Invite unsaved students to receive Christ.
Snack	Jello Cups
Review Game/ Questions	Beach Ball Pass
Craft	Boat Windsocks
Closing	Announcements and Prayer Distribute take-home papers.

Lesson Six Overview

Jesus Calms the Storm

Theme—Jesus is able to rescue me from danger.

Scripture
Mark 4:35–41

Memory Verse
Psalm 46:1—"God is our refuge and strength, a very present help in trouble."

Lesson Outline

Introducing the Story

In today's story, the disciples became very, very scared. What made them scared was a sudden, terrible storm that came while they were on a boat on the Sea of Galilee. Their parents were not with them on that boat. But Jesus was! We can learn from their story that we never need to fear when Jesus is with us.

Telling the Story

1. **A Terrible Storm** (vv. 35–37, John 18:4, 1 John 3:20)
2. **The Fears of the Disciples** (v. 38, Mark 5:36b, 1 Peter 5:7)
3. **Jesus Calmed the Storm** (v. 39, Matthew 28:18)
4. **Two Good Questions** (v. 40)
5. **Jesus is More Than Just a Man!** (v. 41, John 1:3, Colossians 1:16–17)

Applying the Story

Whatever it is that causes fear in your heart and mind, Jesus can rescue you!

6 Lesson Six

Jesus Calms the Storm

Theme: Jesus is able to rescue me from danger.

Scripture

Mark 4:35–41

35 And the same day, when the even was come, he saith unto them, Let us pass over unto the other side.

36 And when they had sent away the multitude, they took him even as he was in the ship. And there were also with him other little ships.

37 And there arose a great storm of wind, and the waves beat into the ship, so that it was now full.

38 And he was in the hinder part of the ship, asleep on a pillow: and they awake him, and say unto him, Master, carest thou not that we perish?

39 And he arose, and rebuked the wind, and said unto the sea, Peace, be still. And the wind ceased, and there was a great calm.

40 And he said unto them, Why are ye so fearful? how is it that ye have no faith?

41 And they feared exceedingly, and said one to another, What manner of man is this, that even the wind and the sea obey him?

Memory Verse

Psalm 46:1
"God is our refuge and strength, a very present help in trouble."

Lesson Six—Jesus Calms the Storm

Teacher's Checklist

- Read Mark 4:35–41 daily
- Study Lesson Six
- Gather for lesson—dry erase marker or chalk
- Prepare snack—Jello cups with gummy fish (such as *Swedish Fish*)
- Gather for object lesson—sunblock
- Gather supplies for review game—beach ball, CD player and CD
- Print this week's memory verse Psalm 46:1 from the Ministry Resource CD
- Purchase for craft—white streamers, blue streamers, and fishing line
- Print for craft— boat scene template from the Ministry Resource CD
- Gather for craft—glue, crayons, scissors, and hole punch
- Print and duplicate Coloring Pages or Activity Pages on the Ministry Resource CD (one per student)
- Print and duplicate Take-Home Paper on the Ministry Resource CD (one per student)

Snack Suggestion

Consider preparing Jello cups for a snack to be served after the lesson. Prepare blue Jello in individual clear cups. Before the Jello stiffens, place gummy fish inside, to give the effect of a miniature sea. Use the stillness of the Jello to explain how Jesus caused the winds and waves to be still.

Lesson Six—Jesus Calms the Storm

Bible Lesson

Teaching Tip

Scripture: Mark 4:35–41

INTRODUCING THE STORY

What scares you the most? Some people are scared of snakes, some of spiders, some of heights, some of the dark, and some of water (even calm water). In scary situations, who usually helps you? Sometimes parents will hold their child's hand when he is scared. Sometimes parents will just "be with" their child when she is scared, and the simple fact that mom or dad is there takes the fear away.

In today's story, the disciples became very, very scared. What made them scared was a sudden, terrible storm that came while they were on a boat on the Sea of Galilee. Their parents were not with them on that boat. But Jesus was! We can learn from their story that we never need to fear when Jesus is with us. He is able to rescue us from every danger.

THE STORY

1. A Terrible Storm (vv. 35–37)

Jesus had been preaching and doing miracles all day and wanted to travel by boat to the other side of the Sea of Galilee. This was a trip that Peter, Andrew, James, and John would have taken many times before. These four disciples (two pairs of brothers) were fishermen on the Sea of Galilee before they became followers of Jesus.

Even though the disciples did not know what was going to happen on the sea that day, you probably do! How do you know? Probably because you have heard this story before! Do you know who else knew this storm was coming? Jesus! You don't think the storm surprised Jesus, do you? Since Jesus was God, He knew everything, including the fact that a storm was on the way. The Bible teaches this:

John 18:4
4   *Jesus therefore, knowing all things that should come upon him, went forth, and said unto them, Whom seek ye?*

Create a "storm" in your classroom by dividing your students into four groups. (The students must not talk or make additional noise for this to work effectively.) The first group rubs both hands together to create the sound of wind. After a few seconds, the second group snaps with both hands to create the sound of rain. The third group of students then begins to pat their legs with their hands, creating the sound of louder rain and bigger rain drops. The final group stomps their feet to make the sound of thunder. Allow them to do this for a few seconds to experience what a thunderstorm could sound like. Have the students stop the storm slowly by ceasing their actions in reverse order.

Draw It!

The Signs of Our Saviour | © 2009 Striving Together Publications

Lesson Six—Jesus Calms the Storm

Draw It!

1 John 3:20

20 For if our heart condemn us, God is greater than our heart, and knoweth all things.

Now that we know that Jesus knew about the storm, notice what Jesus said to the disciples: "Let us pass over unto the other side" (verse 35). Jesus knew about the storm, and He also knew that they would come through the storm safely. He told the disciples that He had every intention of safely arriving on the other side.

Draw It!

2. The Fears of the Disciples (v. 38)

After having seen Jesus turn water into wine, heal the sick, and even raise the dead, the disciples should have known that they had nothing to fear, since He had promised to arrive at the other side.

Sometimes fear causes us to question what God has said in His Word. In our minds, we know the promises of God. But in the middle of a difficult situation, we seem to forget, and we question Him. That is what the disciples did.

See what Jesus said to a man whose daughter was very sick, whom He had promised to heal:

Mark 5:36b

36 …he saith unto the ruler of the synagogue, Be not afraid, only believe.

You see, when we are faced with difficulty or a scary situation, we have two choices: We can be afraid, or we can believe. We cannot do both.

Can you think of some promises God has made to us in His Word that we need to remember and believe?

- God loves us. (1 John 3:1)
- God will never leave us. (Hebrews 13:5)
- God will protect us. (John 10:28–29)
- God will provide for us. (Matthew 6:33)
- God will help us to overcome sin and temptation. (1 Corinthians 10:13)

The disciples forgot what Jesus had said and became so scared that they went to find Him. Now, Jesus was asleep. Doesn't that make you smile, to think that while everyone else was running around panicking, our Saviour was not at all worried? He was asleep, peacefully confident in the fact that He and His Father were in charge.

The disciples asked Jesus whether He cared that they were about to die. We are like the disciples sometimes—we question whether God loves us or cares for us. But we should never make this mistake because His Word says:

1 Peter 5:7

7 *Casting all your care upon him; for he careth for you.*

If God was willing to send Jesus, His Son, to die on the Cross for us, He has proven once and for all that He cares about and loves us.

3. Jesus Calmed the Storm (v. 39)

As simply and easily as could be, Jesus stood up and said, "Peace, be still." And with just a few words, this huge sea became calm. The rain, thunder, lightning, and wind all stopped…immediately!

Usually in nature, when a storm over a lake finally ends, it takes some hours for the water to return to calm and for the waves to flatten out. But this day on the Sea of Galilee, the calm didn't take an hour or two, or even five minutes. It occurred immediately. This was no hard task for the Son of God, the Creator of the world, and the One to whom had been given "all power."

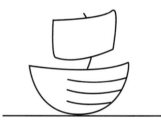

Matthew 28:18

18 *And Jesus came and spake unto them, saying, All power is given unto me in heaven and in earth.*

The word "power" in Matthew 28:18 refers to authority. In other words, Jesus has authority over everything. He is always "in charge!"

4. Two Good Questions (v. 40)

After calming the storm, Jesus turned to the disciples, and asked two questions:

Lesson Six—Jesus Calms the Storm

1. "Why are ye so fearful?" The next time you're scared, think of Jesus asking you this question. After all He has done for you, after showing His love and proving His power, do you really have anything to fear?

2. "How is it that ye have no faith?" The next time you wonder whether Jesus can solve a problem or rescue you from danger, think of Jesus asking you this question. Jesus has power over this world and everything that is in it. And we can have faith in Him—that He is working all things together for our good. But we must have faith to believe this.

5. Jesus Is More Than Just a Man! (v. 41)

The disciples had never seen the sea or the wind obey a man's instructions. They wondered what kind of man Jesus was! They already knew that He was more than just a man. But maybe, they did not realize how much more than a man He really was. The Scripture says the disciples feared, but now, the kind of fear they had was respect and reverence for the powerful Lord whom even the winds and the sea obeyed!

John 1:3
3   All things were made by him; and without him was not any thing made that was made.

Since Jesus created the seas, He had the authority and power to calm them in a moment at His instruction. All of creation is held together by Him and is under His control.

Colossians 1:16–17
16   For by him were all things created, that are in heaven, and that are in earth, visible and invisible, whether they be thrones, or dominions, or principalities, or powers: all things were created by him, and for him:
17   And he is before all things, and by him all things consist.

APPLYING THE STORY

Whatever it is that causes fear in your heart and mind, Jesus can rescue you! The next time you are afraid or someone you know is afraid, what will you do because of what we learned in today's lesson?

- Maybe you could encourage a friend or a member of your family who has a problem or who is scared. You could tell them, "Jesus is in charge, and He promises to take care of us!"
- Maybe you should spend more time in Bible reading, to be more aware of God's promises and to strengthen your faith. Romans 10:17 teaches that our faith is produced by hearing the Word of God.
- Maybe you've been worried and frustrated about a problem. Maybe you've even been upset at the Lord and wondered whether He cares for you. If so, you should ask Him to forgive you for your doubt and to help you trust Him more.

Lesson Six—Jesus Calms the Storm

Beach Ball Pass

Materials Needed
- CD player with CD (perhaps a nature thunderstorm CD)
- Small beach ball or toy boat

Instructions

Explain that this game is like musical chairs. Have all students stand. You will be passing an object, and when the music stops, the person holding the object will answer the question. If the student answers the question correctly they stay in the game. If the student answers incorrectly, they will sit down.

Optional: Present all students who are still standing a sticker or piece of candy.

1. What time of day does our lesson take place?
   Answer: Evening

2. What had Jesus been doing on that "same day"?
   Answer: Teaching and performing miracles

3. Where does our lesson take place?
   Answer: On a ship in the sea

4. On what sea are they sailing?
   Answer: The Sea of Galilee

5. What was the storm like?
   Answer: It was a great storm. It was sudden (no warning) with terrible winds and harsh waves.

6. What was Jesus doing during the storm?
   Answer: Sleeping

7. What was the reaction of the disciples when they saw Jesus sleeping?
   Answer: They asked if He cared that they were going to die.

8. Did the disciples ask Jesus to calm the storm?
   Answer: No

9. What did Jesus do?
   Answer: He calmed the storm.

10. How did the disciples' fear before the storm differ from their fear after the storm?
    Answer: Before the storm they were afraid. After the storm they were in awe and reverence.

Teaching the Memory Verse

Psalm 46:1

1 *God is our refuge and strength, a very present help in trouble.*

As you explain each card (print from Ministry Resource CD), have a student come to the front and hold it.

"God is our refuge"—Refuge is a place of protection.

"and strength"—Not only does He protect us, but He gives us strength!

"a very present"—He is with us all the time.

"help in trouble"—We can know that when troubles come, He will be there to help, protect and strengthen us—what a great promise.

Use companion flashcards found in Visual Resource Packet or images found on Ministry Resource CD.

Lesson Six—Jesus Calms the Storm

Object Lesson—God's Protection

Materials Needed:
Sunblock

Lesson:
I hear all the time how being exposed to the sun can be harmful to us. It can damage the skin and even cause cancer. That's pretty scary! So, before I go out in the sun, I apply this (hold up the sunscreen). How many of you have used sunscreen before? Good.

Sunscreen can protect us from the dangerous rays of the sun. But we have to apply it.

Application:
In other areas of our life, we can experience danger and fear as well. Maybe you have a fear of heights, spiders, or death. The cure for our fears is to walk closely with God (just as we would apply sun screen closely to our skin). God is bigger and more powerful than anything that might scare us. We need to let God do His work in us.

Additional Resources

Find the following items on the Ministry Resource CD:
- Coloring Page (for younger children)
- Activity Page (for older children)
- Student Take-Home Paper
- PowerPoint Presentation

Craft—Boat Windsocks

Getting It Together

White streamers
Blue streamers
Glue
Scissors
Hole punch
Fishing Line
Crayons

Per student:
1   20 inch piece of yarn, fishing line, or ribbon
1   boat scene template located on the resource CD
3   18-inch, blue streamers
3   18-inch, white streamers

Putting It Together

1. Print and cut out 1 boat scene template for each student.
2. Have the students color the boat scene.
3. Glue (You can also tape or staple.) the ends of the scene to each other, forming a cylinder shape.
4. Each student should have 6 total streamers, 18 inches in length, 3 blue and 3 white.
5. Glue (or tape) each streamer to the inside bottom of the boat scene, alternating the colors.
6. Hole punch a single hole on opposites sides of the top of the boat scene.
7. Run the yarn, fishing line, or ribbon through the holes to form a triangle for the windsock to hang from.

Seeing It Together

When the storms of life blow, we can trust Jesus, Who has the power to calm the storms and protect us in trouble.

Suggested Classroom Schedule

Before Class		Complete attendance record. Provide students with coloring pages/activity pages.
Opening		Welcome
Prayer		Prayer requests and praise reports from the children
Song Time		
Memory Verse		2 Corinthians 5:17
Song Time		
Object Lesson		What Change!
Bible Lesson		Jesus Sets a Maniac Free
Application/Invitation		Help saved students apply lesson. Invite unsaved students to receive Christ.
Snack		Butterfly Treat
Review Game/ Questions		PIG
Craft		Chain
Closing		Announcements and Prayer Distribute take-home papers.

Lesson Seven Overview

Jesus Sets a Maniac Free

Theme—Jesus changes people's lives.

Scripture
Mark 5:1–20

Memory Verse
2 Corinthians 5:17—*"Therefore if any man be in Christ, he is a new creature: old things are passed away; behold, all things are become new."*

Lesson Outline

Introducing the Story

Today's story picks up where we left off last week. The disciples and Jesus arrived safely at the other side of the Sea of Galilee. The first person they met there was a very unusual man. And they were about to see the amazing change that could occur in someone's life, all because of Jesus.

Telling the Story

1. A Scary Man in a Cemetery (vv. 1–7)—*Flash Card 7.1*

2. **Jesus Sends the Demons out of the Man** (vv. 8–10, *Ephesians 1:13*)

3. **The Demons Enter Nearby Pigs** (vv. 11–13, 1 Peter 5:8, *John 10:10*)—*Flash Card 7.2*

4. **The People Find a Changed Man** (vv. 14–17, *2 Corinthians 5:17*)—*Flash Card 7.3*

5. **The Man Tells His Friends about Jesus** (vv. 18–20)

Applying the Story

Jesus has the power to set us free from our sin!

7 Lesson Seven

Jesus Sets a Maniac Free

Theme: Jesus changes people's lives.

Scripture

Mark 5:1–20

1 And they came over unto the other side of the sea, into the country of the Gadarenes.
2 And when he was come out of the ship, immediately there met him out of the tombs a man with an unclean spirit,
3 Who had his dwelling among the tombs; and no man could bind him, no, not with chains:
4 Because that he had been often bound with fetters and chains, and the chains had been plucked asunder by him, and the fetters broken in pieces: neither could any man tame him.
5 And always, night and day, he was in the mountains, and in the tombs, crying, and cutting himself with stones.
6 But when he saw Jesus afar off, he ran and worshipped him,
7 And cried with a loud voice, and said, What have I to do with thee, Jesus, thou Son of the most high God? I adjure thee by God, that thou torment me not.
8 For he said unto him, Come out of the man, thou unclean spirit.
9 And he asked him, What is thy name? And he answered, saying, My name is Legion: for we are many.
10 And he besought him much that he would not send them away out of the country.
11 Now there was there nigh unto the mountains a great herd of swine feeding.
12 And all the devils besought him, saying, Send us into the swine, that we may enter into them.
13 And forthwith Jesus gave them leave. And the unclean spirits went out, and entered into the swine: and the herd ran violently down a steep place into the sea, (they were about two thousand;) and were choked in the sea.
14 And they that fed the swine fled, and told it in the city, and in the country. And they went out to see what it was that was done.
15 And they come to Jesus, and see him that was possessed with the devil, and had the legion, sitting, and clothed, and in his right mind: and they were afraid.
16 And they that saw it told them how it befell to him that was possessed with the devil, and also concerning the swine.

Memory Verse

2 Corinthians 5:17
"Therefore if any man be in Christ, he is a new creature: old things are passed away; behold, all things are become new."

17 And they began to pray him to depart out of their coasts.
18 And when he was come into the ship, he that had been possessed with the devil prayed him that he might be with him.
19 Howbeit Jesus suffered him not, but saith unto him, Go home to thy friends, and tell them how great things the Lord hath done for thee, and hath had compassion on thee.
20 And he departed, and began to publish in Decapolis how great things Jesus had done for him: and all men did marvel.

Teacher's Checklist

- ❑ Read Mark 5:1–20 daily
- ❑ Study Lesson Seven
- ❑ Flashcards 7.1—7.3
- ❑ Prepare snack—butterfly treats
- ❑ Object lesson—What Change!
- ❑ Print and cut out "PIG" review game from Ministry Resource CD
- ❑ Print this week's memory verse (2 Corinthians 5:17) from the Ministry Resource CD
- ❑ Purchase for craft—construction paper
- ❑ Print for craft—verse template from the Ministry Resource CD
- ❑ Gather for craft—glue and scissors f
- ❑ Print and duplicate Coloring Pages or Activity Pages on the Ministry Resource CD (one per student)
- ❑ Print and duplicate Take-Home Paper on the Ministry Resource CD (one per student)

Butterfly Treat
Just as the caterpillar changes into a butterfly, Jesus can make all things new! To make this snack, slightly melt caramel candy on a silicone mat on a cookie sheet. Quickly add two twisty pretzels to form wings and add two chocolate chips for the eyes. For a healthier version: Cut celery into approximately two inch pieces. Fill with cream cheese. Add the pretzels for wings and raisins for eyes.

Bible Lesson

Scripture: Mark 5:1–20

INTRODUCING THE STORY

Have your parents ever told you not to talk to strangers? This is wise, because some people in this world would harm you if they were given the opportunity. But even if your parents did not give you such a warning, I do not think you would be eager to talk with the man in today's story.

Do you remember that last week the disciples were caught in a storm at sea? Who calmed the storm? Do you think they ever got to the other side?

Today's story picks up where we left off last week. The disciples and Jesus arrived safely at the other side of the Sea of Galilee and were now in the country of the Gadarenes. The first person they met there was not someone the disciples probably expected to meet. They met a very unusual man. And they were about to see the amazing change that occurs in someone's life, all because of Jesus.

THE STORY

1. A Scary Man in a Cemetery (vv. 1–7)

Jesus and the disciples had just gotten off of the boat when a very strange and scary man approached them. The Bible says that this man lived among the tombs. This is where dead bodies were buried. It would be like living in the middle of a cemetery! I don't know anyone who would want to sleep outside, under the trees, with people's graves all around them.

This man had tremendous problems. In a few minutes I'll explain why he acted the way he did, but first let's see what the Bible says about him. This man would walk back and forth between the cemetery and the nearby mountains each day. As he went, he would scream, shout, moan, and groan. He would take sharp rocks and cut himself, causing his body to bleed.

He was so wild and dangerous, that people who lived near him tried to control him several times by placing chains on his hands and feet. Do you know what happened when they did that? He was so strong that he broke the chains every time. It makes me wonder how they got the chains on him. The Bible does not say, but maybe they placed the chains on him while he

Lesson Seven—Jesus Sets a Maniac Free

Flash Card 7.1

was sleeping. But when Jesus got off of the boat on the shore of the Sea of Galilee, this man came running to Jesus, and fell at His feet. You might wonder what would cause such a wild man to respond to Jesus in this way.

2. Jesus Sends the Demons out of the Man (vv. 8–10)

The Bible says this man had an "unclean spirit" living inside of him. This means that demons were living inside the man's body.

You see, in this world, there are invisible angels and demons. God created these special beings before He created Adam and Eve.

At first they were all good, heavenly angels. But one of those angels, Lucifer, chose to rebel against God. He wanted the worship that only God the Father was to receive. And one-third of all angels followed him in his wicked rebellion against God. Because of this, all of them were removed from Heaven. The devil and those demons that help him will eventually be bound, and then cast into the Lake of Fire, to be punished forever (Revelation 20:10). But until then, God has allowed them to roam about invisibly in this world (Ephesians 2:2, 6:12). Angels go about doing good on the earth, and demons go about doing evil.

The demons inside the man were controlling his words and actions. These demons immediately knew who Jesus was when He arrived (James 2:19). They fell down at His feet asking Him for mercy. They knew they could not hide, because Jesus knew everything. So they came to Jesus within this man's body and asked Him not to torment or punish them.

Jesus said, "Come out of the man, thou unclean spirit." Jesus also asked the name of the demon inside of the man. A demon answered with the name "Legion," because there were actually many demons inside this man's body.

If you have received Jesus Christ as your Saviour, you do not need to worry about a demon living inside of you, as they lived inside of this man. Why? Because the Holy Spirit already lives inside of you. He has moved in and locked the door, so no evil spirit can enter! The Bible calls this the "sealing" of the Holy Spirit. We can be thankful for this.

Ephesians 1:13

13   In whom ye also trusted, after that ye heard the word of truth, the gospel of your salvation: in whom also after that ye believed, ye were sealed with that holy Spirit of promise,

3. The Demons Enter Nearby Pigs (vv. 11–13)

The idea the demons had was that if they had to leave the man, they could enter into a herd of pigs nearby. Jesus gave the command, and the demons left the man and filled the pigs. There were about two thousand pigs. When the demons entered the pigs, they went crazy, just as the man had been crazy before, and they ran down a hill, right into the Sea of Galilee.

We should remember that the devil and his demons are always involved in ruining people's lives and hurting them. The devil tries to trick us to sin and to do wicked things. But the result of following him is always destruction.

1 Peter 5:8

8   *Be sober, be vigilant; because your adversary the devil, as a roaring lion, walketh about, seeking whom he may devour:*

Jesus, on the other hand, is always involved in making people's lives better and filling them with joy. When we choose to follow Jesus, instead of the devil, we can know that He has blessings in store for us!

John 10:10

10 *The thief cometh not, but for to steal, and to kill, and to destroy: I am come that they might have life, and that they might have it more abundantly.*

4. The People Find a Changed Man (vv. 14–17)

The men who had been feeding the pigs in the field near where Jesus was had never seen anything like this! They could see Jesus and this maniac in the distance talking with each other. Then, out of nowhere, all of their pigs went crazy and ran into the sea, drowning themselves. (You know, pigs can't swim!) They could hardly believe their eyes.

Since the men had no more pigs to feed, they ran into the city to tell their friends what happened. The people decided that they would need to come and see for themselves what had happened off the shore of the Sea of Galilee.

Flash Card 7.3

When the people from the city arrived to where Jesus and the man were, they were amazed. They were not amazed by the fact that all the pigs were gone, but by the change in this man. You see, everyone knew about this crazy man who lived among the tombs. He was famous. But now there he was, "sitting, and clothed, and in his right mind." He was no longer a scary, out of control man. He was calm, he was quiet, and he was listening to Jesus.

2 Corinthians 5:17

17 *Therefore if any man be in Christ, he is a new creature: old things are passed away; behold, all things are become new.*

5. The Man Tells His Friends about Jesus (vv. 18–20)

Instead of being thankful, the people were confused and scared. Maybe the people who owned sheep and cows wondered whether Jesus was going to cause their animals to run into the sea. Maybe they figured anyone who had a relationship with this maniac was someone they could not trust. For whatever reason, they came to Jesus, and asked Him to leave their town.

As Jesus entered the boat to leave, the man asked if he could go with Jesus. You can understand how thankful this man was to Jesus for sending the demons out of him!

But Jesus answered that instead of going with them, the man should "Go home to thy friends, and tell them how great things the Lord hath done for thee."

APPLYING THE STORY

What has Jesus done for you that you can tell someone about? He has done great things for each of us. He died on the Cross to pay for our sins. He has given us health and families. He has given us a church and teachers to teach about Him. We should tell others how good He has been to us!

Lesson Seven—Jesus Sets a Maniac Free

Is your life different because you know Jesus than it would be if you did not know Him? The change this man experienced was obvious to those who lived in his city.

We should "show and tell" our faith in Jesus! Our lips *tell* people about our faith in Him. And our lives *show* people about our faith in Him. This is God's plan. James said, "I will shew thee my faith by my works" (James 2:18).

Lesson Seven—Jesus Sets a Maniac Free

 # Review Game/Questions

"PIG"

Materials Needed
- Visual for "PIG"—found on the Ministry Resource CD

Instructions
Print and cut out the visual for "PIG." Place all squares, blank side up, on the chalk tray (or tape to the board). Today, it is the class against the teacher! Ask the class a question, and call on a student to answer. If the student answers correctly, they may pick a square from the chalk tray. The goal is to pick a smiley face. If they pick a square with a pig on it, write the letter "P" on the board. Continue asking questions. If they select another pig, write the letter "I". If they pick a third pig, write the letter "G". The goal is to not spell "PIG." If the class does not spell "PIG" after all the questions are asked, the class wins a piece of candy. If they spell "pig," the teacher wins and keeps the candy.

1. After the storm, where did Jesus land?
   Answer: Country of the Gadarenes

2. Who greeted Jesus as He got off the boat?
   Answer: A man with an unclean spirit

3. Where did this man live?
   Answer: In the tombs (or cemetery)

4. What had been done to the maniac to subdue him?
   Answer: He was bound with fetters and chains

5. How did the maniac act?
   Answer: He cried and cut himself.

6. What did the maniac say when Jesus asked his name?
   Answer: "Legion, for we are many."

7. Where did the demons say they wanted to go?
   Answer: Into a herd of swine (pigs)

8. What happened to the pigs when the unclean spirits entered them?
   Answer: They ran off a steep cliff and drowned in the sea.

9. What happened to the man?
   Answer: He was free of the unclean spirits. He was sitting, clothed, and in his right mind.

10. The man wanted to go on the ship with Jesus, instead Jesus gave him another job. What was it?
    Answer: Go home to thy friends and tell them how great things the Lord hath done.

Teaching the Memory Verse

2 Corinthians 5:17
17 Therefore if any man be in Christ, he is a new creature: old things are passed away; behold, all things are become new.

As you explain each card (print from Ministry Resource CD), have a student come to the front and hold it.

"Therefore if any man be in Christ"—What does it mean to be in Christ? When we accept Jesus Christ as our Saviour we are "in Christ". This would be a good time to pause and explain the Gospel message in detail.

"he is a new creature"—He is now free from the bondage of sin.

"old things are passed away"—Our former view and feelings of spiritual things have changed.

"behold, all things are become new"—God gives us new affections and a new spiritual appetite.

Use companion flashcards found in Visual Resource Packet or images found on Ministry Resource CD.

Lesson Seven—Jesus Sets a Maniac Free

Object Lesson—What Change!

Materials Needed:

- "Magic Pen" marker (Crayola makes one called "Color Changeable Markers")
- Paper

Lesson:

As you are talking, write your name or just the word "me" on the paper so students can see. Then go over what you just wrote with the "Color Change Wand." The original color will change to a new color.

Show the students the magic marker. Many of you have seen and even used one of these pens. Aren't they the neatest things? You write in one color and then the "Color Change Wand" changes the color to a brand new color…not a lighter shade, but a whole new color!

Application:

That is what Jesus does with us! When we accept Christ as our Saviour, He takes this old sinful body and gives us a new nature! What a change!

Lesson Seven—Jesus Sets a Maniac Free

Craft—Chain

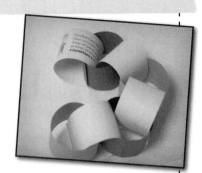

Getting It Together

White cardstock or construction paper
Scissors
Glue

Per Student:
1   verse template link located on the resource CD for each student

Putting It Together

1. Print on white cardstock and cut out the chain link verse template for each student (2"x 6"). This will be the first link in the chain.
2. Glue the ends of the strip of paper together to form a circle shape.
3. Cut several other blank strips of construction paper (2" x 8") to form the rest of the chain.

Seeing It Together

Jesus can help free us from the sins of life.

Additional Resources

Find the following items on the Ministry Resource CD:
- Coloring Page (for younger children)
- Activity Page (for older children)
- Student Take-Home Paper
- PowerPoint Presentation

The Signs of Our Saviour | © 2009 Striving Together Publications

Suggested Classroom Schedule

Before Class	Complete attendance record. Provide students with coloring pages/activity pages.
Opening	Welcome
Prayer	Prayer requests and praise reports from the children
Song Time	
Memory Verse	Ephesians 3:20
Song Time	
Object Lesson	Our Invisible Helper
Bible Lesson	Jesus Heals a Sick Woman
Application/Invitation	Help saved students apply lesson. Invite unsaved students to receive Christ.
Snack	Stethoscope Snack
Review Game/ Questions	Pick-a-Point
Craft	Jesus "Washes" away my sins
Closing	Announcements and Prayer Distribute take-home papers.

Lesson Eight Overview

Jesus Heals a Sick Woman

Theme—Jesus can help me when others are unable.

Scripture
Mark 5:24–34

Memory Verse
Ephesians 3:20—"Now unto him that is able to do exceeding abundantly above all that we ask or think, according to the power that worketh in us,"

Lesson Outline

Introducing the Story
Today we will learn about a lady who was sick for twelve years! Thankfully, this lady lived during the time when Jesus was here on earth and was performing the wonderful miracles about which we have been learning. Let's look into our Bibles to see what happened on the special day when Jesus came through her city.

Telling the Story
1. **A Very Crowded Street** (v. 24)
2. **A Very Sick Woman** (vv. 25–26, Luke 7:16–17)
3. **The Woman Is Healed by Touching Jesus' Clothes** (vv. 27–29, Psalm 92:4)
4. **Jesus Asks a Surprising Question** (vv. 30–32)
5. **Jesus Explains the Importance of Her Faith** (vv. 33–34, Acts 4:12, Hebrews 11:6)

Applying the Story (Romans 10:9)
Is there something in your life that you need Jesus' help with? Maybe there's a problem in your family, or with someone you know. Do you believe that Jesus can help? Will you come to Him in faith, through prayer, and ask Him to meet the need?

8 Lesson Eight

Jesus Heals a Sick Woman

Theme: Jesus can help me when others are unable.

Scripture

Mark 5:24–34

24 And Jesus went with him; and much people followed him, and thronged him.
25 And a certain woman, which had an issue of blood twelve years,
26 And had suffered many things of many physicians, and had spent all that she had, and was nothing bettered, but rather grew worse,
27 When she had heard of Jesus, came in the press behind, and touched his garment.
28 For she said, If I may touch but his clothes, I shall be whole.
29 And straightway the fountain of her blood was dried up; and she felt in her body that she was healed of that plague.
30 And Jesus, immediately knowing in himself that virtue had gone out of him, turned him about in the press, and said, Who touched my clothes?
31 And his disciples said unto him, Thou seest the multitude thronging thee, and sayest thou, Who touched me?
32 And he looked round about to see her that had done this thing.
33 But the woman fearing and trembling, knowing what was done in her, came and fell down before him, and told him all the truth.
34 And he said unto her, Daughter, thy faith hath made thee whole; go in peace, and be whole of thy plague.

Memory Verse

Ephesians 3:20
"Now unto him that is able to do exceeding abundantly above all that we ask or think, according to the power that worketh in us,"

Lesson Eight—Jesus Heals a Sick Woman

Teacher's Checklist

- ❑ Read Mark 5:24–34 daily
- ❑ Study Lesson Eight
- ❑ Prepare snack—Stethoscope (using Twizzlers and marshmallows)
- ❑ Gather for object lesson—deflated balloon, ball, and flotation device
- ❑ Print and cut out "Pick-a-Point" review game from Ministry Resource CD
- ❑ Print this week's memory verse (Ephesians 3:20) from the Ministry Resource CD
- ❑ Purchase for craft—child-size hanger, clothes pins, felt, denim fabric, and chenille
- ❑ Print for craft—verse template from the Ministry Resource CD
- ❑ Print for craft—boy template from the Ministry Resource CD
- ❑ Print for craft—shirt and pant template from the "Ministry Resource CD
- ❑ Gather for craft—glue, scissors, and crayons for craft
- ❑ Print and duplicate Coloring Pages or Activity Pages on the Ministry Resource CD (one per student)
- ❑ Print and duplicate Take-Home Paper on the Ministry Resource CD (one per student)

Snack Suggestion

Make a stethoscope out of Pull-n-Peel Twizzlers. You'll need small marshmallows, large marshmallows, and Pull-n-Peel Twizzlers.

Pull apart the Pull-n-Peel Twizzler, giving each student 2 Twizzler strings. Insert 1 small marshmallow in one end of each of the 2 Twizzler strings. Twist the bottom half of the 2 strings together. Insert 1 large marshmallow in the end of the twisted Twizzlers to form a stethoscope.

Lesson Eight—Jesus Heals a Sick Woman

 # Bible Lesson

Scripture: Mark 5:24–34

INTRODUCING THE STORY

Have you recently been sick? No one likes to be sick. You might like to miss a day of school. But I would guess that when you're sick, you'd rather be at school with your friends than at home and miserable.

When I am sick, it seems like it takes forever for me to get well. Usually being sick only lasts for a few days. But those few days seem to drag on and take much longer than other normal days.

Today we will learn about a lady who was sick for twelve years! I can't imagine being as sick as this lady. Thankfully, this lady lived during the time when Jesus was here on earth performing the wonderful miracles about which we have been learning. Let's look into our Bibles to see what happened on the special day when Jesus came through her city.

THE STORY

1. A Very Crowded Street (v. 24)

Last week we ended our story with Jesus getting on a boat, after having sent many demons out of a man, who was now very thankful. That man went to tell his friends, and Jesus came back to the other side (the west side) of the Sea of Galilee.

As Jesus left the boat and stepped on shore, immediately a great crowd gathered around Him. Everyone seemed to want to hear what Jesus would have to say. And many had needs, for which they would ask His help.

A man named Jairus was in the first group to meet Jesus. He asked Jesus to come to his home and to heal his sick daughter. Jesus agreed, and they began to walk together toward the man's house. But the crowd remained large. People were pushing and shoving each other to get closer to Jesus.

You may have experienced a crowd like this at an amusement park, or while at a shopping mall, or in the downtown of a large city, or at an airport, or on a crowded trolley-car or bus. (Allow students to give examples.)

Use a Bible-times map to explain the location of Jesus.

The Signs of Our Saviour | © 2009 Striving Together Publications   99

Lesson Eight—Jesus Heals a Sick Woman

2. A Very Sick Woman (vv. 25–26)

In the crowd that day was a woman who had heard of Jesus. She had heard about the miracles He performed and the great power He had. How do you think she heard about Jesus? (Allow students to answer.) Do you remember, from our lesson three weeks ago, when Jesus raised the man from the dead in the city of Nain? What happened at the end of the story? Many people began telling their friends in different cities about how amazing and powerful Jesus was.

> **Luke 7:16–17**
> 16 *And there came a fear on all: and they glorified God, saying, That a great prophet is risen up among us; and, That God hath visited his people.*
> 17 *And this rumour of him went forth throughout all Judaea, and throughout all the region round about.*

This woman had heard about this miracle and others. Maybe she thought to herself, "If He could raise up a man who was dead, then He could certainly heal me of my sickness." She determined, if she could get just close enough to to touch Jesus' clothes, that she could be healed (verse 28).

The Bible says she had "an issue of blood." This means that her sickness was inside of her body, as part of her bloodstream. Because of this, she experienced great pain throughout her body. Her sickness also caused her body to bleed, making her very weak.

Getting to Jesus was her last hope, since she had already spent all of her money on many different doctors. She had no money left. In fact, as she continued to spend her money, seeing different doctors and trying different medicines, she only became more and more sick. She figured that the only person who could help her was Jesus. And she was correct!

Act It Out

Large Crowd
Have students gather closely around the teacher. Ask a smaller student in the middle to try to reach the teacher—showing how difficult it would be for this woman to get to Jesus.

3. The Woman Is Healed by Touching Jesus' Clothes (vv. 27–29)

Imagine the excitement that the woman experienced as she saw Jesus coming near to where she was. Though she was weak and in pain, she was not going to allow this crowd to prevent her from getting to Jesus.

Finally, she reached out and touched Jesus' clothing. Immediately, the Bible says, she knew that she was healed. She could feel the pain leave her body. Imagine how happy she must have been!

Psalm 92:4
4   *For thou, LORD, hast made me glad through thy work: I will triumph in the works of thy hands.*

You might expect the story to end here. You might expect Jesus to continue walking through the crowd toward Jairus' house. And you might expect the woman to leave that place and rush home to give her family and friends the wonderful news. But there is more that happened, and we can learn some important lessons.

4. Jesus Asks a Surprising Question (vv. 30–32)

Jesus was being bumped and run into by many people. But when this particular woman touched Him, He knew something different had happened. He knew that the power He possessed, as God's Son, had been used to heal someone.

So Jesus turned and asked, "Who touched my clothes?" His disciples were surprised that He would ask such a question on a crowded street as this one. They were thinking, "What do you mean, 'Who touched me?' Everyone is touching you!"

Do you think, from what you have learned about Jesus, that He already knew exactly who it was that touched Him? I believe He did. So why did He ask? He wanted the miracle this woman had received to be used to teach her, and others, including us, an important lesson.

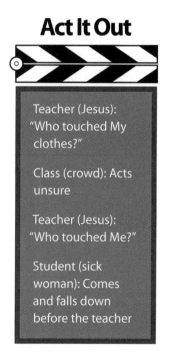

Act It Out

Teacher (Jesus): "Who touched My clothes?"

Class (crowd): Acts unsure

Teacher (Jesus): "Who touched Me?"

Student (sick woman): Comes and falls down before the teacher

5. Jesus Explains the Importance of Her Faith (vv. 33–34)

Jesus wanted her, His disciples, the people on the busy street, and us, to understand exactly why this woman was healed. She was healed for two reasons:

First, she was healed because she came to the right Person. She came to Jesus. No doctors could cure her disease. No ordinary man could heal her. Only Jesus could. Still today, only Jesus is able to heal people from their sins.

> **Acts 4:12**
> 12 *Neither is there salvation in any other: for there is none other name under heaven given among men, whereby we must be saved.*

Teaching Tip

Explain to students that Jesus is the "only way" (John 14:6) to be healed spiritually. Ask older students if they know of other false ways some people try to use as a means of salvation.

Second, she was healed because she had faith in Him. When she placed her faith in doctors, she was disappointed. When she placed her faith in medicine, she only became sicker. Good doctors are a blessing to receive help from, and the right medicine can be used by the Lord to help us feel better. But that is not where we should place our faith. Our faith must be in Jesus.

In this story, Jesus wanted everyone to know that when we place our faith in Him, we will receive His blessings.

> **Hebrews 11:6**
> 6 *But without faith it is impossible to please him: for he that cometh to God must believe that he is, and that he is a rewarder of them that diligently seek him.*

When it comes to seeing our needs met, we are told to come to God in faith. This simply means that we need to believe from our hearts that He is able to meet our needs.

APPLYING THE STORY

Is there something in your life that you need Jesus' help with? Maybe there's a problem in your family or with someone you know. Do you believe that Jesus can help? Will you come to Him in faith, through prayer, and ask Him to meet the need?

Our greatest need is the forgiveness of our sins. And, just as the woman with the issue of blood, when we come to Jesus for this need, we must come in faith. To "have faith" means to "believe." We must believe that He is God's Son, that He went to the Cross of Calvary for us, that He rose from the grave, and that only He can save us and take us to Heaven. Notice what the Bible says about how we come to Him for salvation, with a heart that believes:

Romans 10:9

9   *That if thou shalt confess with thy mouth the Lord Jesus, and shalt believe in thine heart that God hath raised him from the dead, thou shalt be saved.*

How can you "reach out and touch" Jesus today, in faith?

- By asking Him to be your Saviour, if you have never done so
- By reading His Word, the Bible, and being reminded of His goodness and promises
- By spending time in prayer, asking Him to meet your needs, and the needs of others

Review Game/Questions

"Pick-A-Point"

Materials Needed
Visual for "Pick-A-Point" game found on Ministry Resource CD.

Instructions
Print and cut out "Pick-A-Point." Hold the strips in your hand. (Fan the strips out keeping the point values hidden.) Divide the class into teams. Alternate asking questions between the teams. When a student answers a question correctly, that student may pick a point from your hand. The team with the most points wins.

1. How long had this woman been sick?
   Answer: 12 years

2. Was Jesus the first one with whom she sought healing?
   Answer: No, she went to many physicians.

3. How much did she spend trying to get better?
   Answer: All that she had

4. Were doctors and money able to heal her?
   Answer: No, the Bible says she grew worse.

5. What did she want to do when she heard that Jesus was coming?
   Answer: She just wanted to touch His clothes.

6. What happened when she touched His garment?
   Answer: She was immediately healed.

7. What did Jesus say when He knew that virtue had gone out of Him?
   Answer: Who touched me?

8. Why did the disciples think that was such a strange question?
   Answer: Because the crowd was so great. Many people had touched Him.

9. What was the difference with her touch?
   Answer: It was on purpose!

Lesson Eight—Jesus Heals a Sick Woman

10. Did Jesus know who touched Him?
    Answer: Yes

11. Why did He ask the question, "who touched me?"
    Answer: For a testimony to others

12. What did Jesus say had healed the woman?
    Answer: Her faith

 Teaching the Memory Verse

Ephesians 3:20

20   Now unto him that is able to do exceeding abundantly above all that we ask or think, according to the power that worketh in us,

God can do immeasurably more than we can imagine. Give every student (or choose one student) a small measuring cup. Tell the students you are going to fill their cup. Ask them how full they think you will fill it. Fill each cup with candy, cereal, or popcorn. Fill the cup till it overflows and they have to catch the extra. Explain how God does this in even a greater way. God makes things overflow beyond what we can measure or think.

Print the memory verse on cardstock. Call students up to hold the cards. Say the verse several times. Then have your students turn their cards sideways or upside down. The class repeats the verse. Again, have the students turn their card in a different direction and have the class repeats the verse again. Repeat several times.

Use companion flashcards found in Visual Resource Packet or images found on Ministry Resource CD.

Lesson Eight—Jesus Heals a Sick Woman

Object Lesson—Our Invisible Helper

Materials Needed:
- Deflated balloon
- Deflated ball
- Deflated flotation device

Lesson:
Ask the students what these three objects have in common. They all use air. We cannot see the air, but we know it is there because of the effect it has on each of the objects.

Application:
God in His infinite wisdom knew we would need help once He went home to Heaven. So He sent us the Holy Spirit to be our "helper." We cannot see the Holy Spirit, but we know He is working in our lives by the effect He has on us.

Additional Resources

Find the following items on the Ministry Resource CD:
- Coloring Page (for younger children)
- Activity Page (for older children)
- Student Take-Home Paper
- PowerPoint Presentation

Lesson Eight—Jesus Heals a Sick Woman

Craft—Jesus "Washes" Away My Sins

Getting It Together

White Felt
Denim type fabric
Glue
Crayons
Scissors
Child-size hangers
Chenille (hair colors)

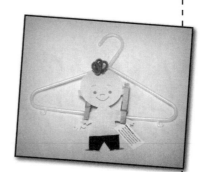

Per student:
1 child-size hanger
1 boy, verse, shirt, and pant template from the resource CD
2 clothes pins

Putting It Together

1. Print the verse and boy template for each student to color.
2. Using the shirt template, trace and cut out the shirts using white felt, gluing the shirt to the boy.
3. Using the pant template, trace and cut out the pants on the blue or denim fabric. (You can use denim patches).
4. Glue the pants to the boy.
5. Roll the ends of the verse sheet to look like a scroll and glue to the boys hand.
6. Using the clothes pens, clip the boy by the middle of his arms to the clothes hanger.

Seeing It Together

Explain to the children that Jesus will wash away our sins if we trust in the Lord Jesus Christ.

Suggested Classroom Schedule

Before Class	Complete attendance record. Provide students with coloring pages/activity pages.
Opening	Welcome
Prayer	Prayer requests and praise reports from the children
Song Time	
Memory Verse	Romans 12:1
Song Time	
Object Lesson	God Can Use Me!
Bible Lesson	Jesus Feeds Five Thousand
Application/Invitation	Help saved students apply lesson. Invite unsaved students to receive Christ.
Snack	Fish-shaped Fruit Snacks
Review Game/ Questions	You Don't Say
Craft	Fish
Closing	Announcements and Prayer Distribute take-home papers.

Lesson Nine Overview

Jesus Feeds Five Thousand

Theme—Give what you have to Jesus and He will use it.

Scripture
John 6:1–14

Memory Verse
Romans 12:1—"I beseech you therefore, brethren, by the mercies of God, that ye present your bodies a living sacrifice, holy, acceptable unto God, which is your reasonable service."

Lesson Outline
Introducing the Story
In the miracle we will study today, we learn about a very large group of people who were very hungry, and how Jesus fed them all with a very small amount of food.

Telling the Story
1. **A Hungry Crowd** (vv. 1–6)
2. **Philip and Andrew Don't Know What to Do** (vv. 7–9)
3. **A Boy Is Willing to Share His Lunch** (v. 9, *Proverbs 3:27–28, James 2:15–16, 1 John 3:17*)
4. **Jesus Multiplies the Food** (vv. 10–11, *Ephesians 3:20*)
5. **Leftovers for the Disciples and Praise for Jesus** (vv. 12–14)

Applying the Story
Do you have something that you think Jesus might want to use? Are you willing to share what you have with Jesus, so that He can use it to bless others? If you make the right choice—like the boy in the story—to share, you will enjoy seeing Jesus use you.

9 Lesson Nine

Jesus Feeds Five Thousand

Theme: Give what you have to Jesus and He will use it.

Scripture

John 6:1–14

1   After these things Jesus went over the sea of Galilee, which is the sea of Tiberias.
2   And a great multitude followed him, because they saw his miracles which he did on them that were diseased.
3   And Jesus went up into a mountain, and there he sat with his disciples.
4   And the passover, a feast of the Jews, was nigh.
5   When Jesus then lifted up his eyes, and saw a great company come unto him, he saith unto Philip, Whence shall we buy bread, that these may eat?
6   And this he said to prove him: for he himself knew what he would do.
7   Philip answered him, Two hundred pennyworth of bread is not sufficient for them, that every one of them may take a little.
8   One of his disciples, Andrew, Simon Peter's brother, saith unto him,
9   There is a lad here, which hath five barley loaves, and two small fishes: but what are they among so many?
10 And Jesus said, Make the men sit down. Now there was much grass in the place. So the men sat down, in number about five thousand.
11 And Jesus took the loaves; and when he had given thanks, he distributed to the disciples, and the disciples to them that were set down; and likewise of the fishes as much as they would.
12 When they were filled, he said unto his disciples, Gather up the fragments that remain, that nothing be lost.
13 Therefore they gathered them together, and filled twelve baskets with the fragments of the five barley loaves, which remained over and above unto them that had eaten.
14 Then those men, when they had seen the miracle that Jesus did, said, This is of a truth that prophet that should come into the world.

Memory Verse

Romans 12:1
"I beseech you therefore, brethren, by the mercies of God, that ye present your bodies a living sacrifice, holy, acceptable unto God, which is your reasonable service."

Lesson Nine—Jesus Feeds Five Thousand

Teacher's Checklist

- ☐ Read John 6:1–14 daily
- ☐ Study Lesson Nine
- ☐ Prepare snack—fish fruit snacks or cheese goldfish crackers
- ☐ Gather for object lesson—Swiss Army knife
- ☐ Print and cut out "You Don't Say" review game from Ministry Resource CD
- ☐ Memory verse (Romans 12:1) from the Visual Resource Packet
- ☐ Print, cut, and mount "Crazy Clown" visual from Ministry Resource CD
- ☐ Purchase for craft—paper plates and wiggly craft eyes
- ☐ Print for craft—verse template from the "Ministry Resource CD
- ☐ Glue, scissors, and paint for craft
- ☐ Print and duplicate Coloring Pages or Activity Pages on the Ministry Resource CD (one per student)
- ☐ Print and duplicate Take-Home Paper on the Ministry Resource CD (one per student)

Serve fruit snacks that come in fish shapes (sharks, etc).

You may also want to serve cheese goldfish crackers.

Lesson Nine—Jesus Feeds Five Thousand

Bible Lesson

Scripture: John 6:1–14

INTRODUCING THE STORY

What is your favorite meal of the day? Is there a time of day when you are more hungry than usual? Many boys and girls are especially hungry when they arrive home from school in the afternoon. Has one of your parents ever told you not to eat a snack, because your family was going to eat dinner in just a few hours? It's hard to wait when you're hungry.

What if you were very hungry, and you or your mother went to the cupboard to find something for you to eat and found nothing? No chips, no cereal, no crackers, no cans of soup…nothing! You might be disappointed. You might think, "This is such an emergency! We should call 911!"

What if you had something very small to eat, and you were hungry, but there were others around who were also hungry and had nothing to eat? Would it be easy for you to share?

In the miracle we will study today, we learn about a very large group of people who were very hungry, and how Jesus fed them all with a very small amount of food.

Teaching Tip

Ask the children in your class what some of their favorite foods are in these categories:

- Cereal
- Dessert
- Pizza
- After school snack
- Ice cream flavor

Teaching Tip

With a younger age group or small class: Bring in a blanket for children to sit on as you tell the lesson, like a picnic.

THE STORY

1. A Hungry Crowd (vv. 1–6)

The more miracles Jesus provided for people, the more people followed Him. When Jesus traveled from city to city or across the Sea of Galilee, as He did several times, people would immediately gather in large crowds to see what He would do or to hear what He would say.

On this day in John chapter 6, Jesus had sailed across the Sea of Galilee and walked up to a nearby mountain with His disciples. Over five thousand people followed them (verse 2) up the mountain.

The Bible tells us that the Passover was about to begin. The Passover was a one-week period when the Jewish people would celebrate what God had done for them many years before. They would gather together with friends and family, much like we might for a birthday or at Christmas. During this celebration, they would eat many meals together. This time reminded

Teaching Tip

Help your students understand how large a group this would have been by providing examples of how many classrooms the size of yours would be filled by this group.

The Signs of Our Saviour | © 2009 Striving Together Publications

111

Lesson Nine—Jesus Feeds Five Thousand

Teacher's Note

"Pharaoh" was the title for the man who ruled Egypt.

them of the time when God kept their families safe during the days of Moses, when God helped them to escape from being slaves in Egypt under the wicked and cruel Pharaoh.

2. Philip and Andrew Don't Know What to Do (vv. 7–9)

Jesus wanted to give the people something to eat. He turned to one of His disciples, Philip, and asked him if he had any ideas where they could buy some food to feed this large group of people. Jesus did not ask this question because He did not know what to do. He asked this question to teach Philip an important lesson about how He could provide for needs, when there didn't seem to be a way. Philip answered that buying enough food for this large crowd would cost far more money than any of them had.

If only half of the men present that day were married, and if each of them had their wives and one child with them (there were probably many more than this), there would have been ten thousand people on the mountain. If we were to purchase a Value Meal for every adult, and a Happy Meal for every child from McDonalds, feeding this many people would cost more than $50,000!

While Philip was explaining to Jesus that they did not have enough money, another disciple, Andrew, informed Jesus that there was one little boy who had some lunch. But how, he asked, could that little lunch ever feed so many people? They were only 9,999 lunches short of what they would need!

Use an Object

Happy Meal
Bring in 2 small fish and 5 rolls. Or, bring in a McDonalds Happy Meal (today's version of the boy's lunch).

3. A Boy Is Willing to Share His Lunch (v. 9)

Among the thousands of people was a little boy who, unlike most of the people, had some food to eat. He was faced with an opportunity to choose between two responses: selfishness or sharing.

Selfishness would choose to keep and protect his food. A selfish young man may have quietly sneaked off to a place where none of the hungry crowd could see him, to eat his lunch alone. He wouldn't have wanted any of the people to know he had a lunch because they might ask him to share.

Lesson Nine—Jesus Feeds Five Thousand

But this boy was not selfish. He chose to share. Consider the following Bible verses which teach us the importance of sharing:

Proverbs 3:27–28

27   *Withhold not good from them to whom it is due, when it is in the power of thine hand to do it.*

28   *Say not unto thy neighbour, Go, and come again, and to morrow I will give; when thou hast it by thee.*

James 2:15–16

15   *If a brother or sister be naked, and destitute of daily food,*

16   *And one of you say unto them, Depart in peace, be ye warmed and filled; notwithstanding ye give them not those things which are needful to the body; what doth it profit?*

1 John 3:17

17   *But whoso hath this world's good, and seeth his brother have need, and shutteth up his bowels of compassion from him, how dwelleth the love of God in him?*

4. Jesus Multiplies the Food (vv. 10–11)

When we are willing to share, Jesus is able to use what we share far more than we would imagine. In this story, Jesus had everyone sit down on the side of the mountain. Then He prayed and thanked His Father for providing the fish and the bread, even though it wasn't very much. By the way, do you remember to thank the Lord before each meal He provides for you?

After everyone had sat down and Jesus had prayed, He began to break up the bread and fish, and then give the food to the disciples to pass out to the people. The disciples were amazed when, as they returned back to get more food for the people, Jesus kept giving more food!

Have you ever been at a meal where your parents told you exactly how much of the food to take because they wanted to be sure there was enough for everyone? Maybe you were told to take only one piece of pizza, or cake, or bread.

The Signs of Our Saviour | © 2009 Striving Together Publications   **113**

But, on the other hand, have you ever been to an "all you can eat" buffet? No matter how much you take, everyone has enough. And it doesn't matter how hungry you are, you can keep coming back for more! That is how it was on that mountain the day that Jesus fed the people. Verse 11 tells us that they had "as much as they would."

Ephesians 3:20

20 Now unto him that is able to do exceeding abundantly above all that we ask or think, according to the power that worketh in us,

5. Leftovers for the Disciples and Praise for Jesus (vv. 12–14)

When we share, as the boy in this story did, not only are people helped, but also we get to enjoy being a part of what Jesus is doing. And on top of that, God receives the glory.

When everyone had been served, Jesus instructed the disciples to go around and collect all the leftovers. Jesus did not want to be wasteful with what His Father had provided.

Can you imagine how strange it was to gather as leftovers more than they even started with? They started with what would fit in about one basket. But there were twelve baskets left over! Maybe each of the disciples was able to keep one basket of bread for the next time he wanted a snack.

The people who were close enough to Jesus to see how everything had happened, could hardly believe what occurred! They realized that Jesus was the Messiah—the One whom God promised would come. When people get close enough to Jesus to experience His greatness and His goodness, they usually choose to believe in Him. That's why we must always work at introducing people to Him.

APPLYING THE STORY

Do you have something that you think Jesus might want to use? Are you willing to share what you have with Jesus so that He can use it to bless others? If you make the right choice—like the boy in the story—to share, you will enjoy seeing Jesus use you.

Lesson Nine—Jesus Feeds Five Thousand

Don't you think the boy in the story enjoyed seeing everyone happily eating and being amazed by how Jesus multiplied the food? He may have been thinking, "How did He do that? How wonderful that He was able to use the little that I gave Him to feed so many!"

Can you give an example of something Jesus would like for you to share with someone else?

- A meal or snack
- An umbrella
- A book or toy
- Your time
- The gospel

Lesson Nine—Jesus Feeds Five Thousand

Review Game/Questions

"You Don't Say"

Materials Needed
Visual for "You Don't Say"—found on the Ministry Resource CD.

Instructions
Divide class into teams. Call on one student from Team A to come to the front. Give one "You Don't Say" card to the student. Tell the student not to let anyone see the card. Now, the student tries to get his/her team to guess the target word or phrase on the card. The student cannot say any word that is in the answer or any of the "do not say" words on the card. These are all words or phrases from today's lesson. The student can repeat any part of the lesson as long as he/she does not say any of the "do not say" words. If the student slips and says a word, his/her turn is over and the "You Don't Say" card goes back into the deck. Each team has one minute to guess the word or phrase. Repeat with Team B.

	Target Word	"You Don't Say" Words
1.	Sea of Galilee	Water, Boat, Lake
2.	Passover	Jewish, Week, Moses
3.	Philip	Disciple, Food, Money
4.	Andrew	Disciple, Boy, Lunch
5.	Sharing	Boy, Fish, Bread
6.	Five loaves and two fishes	Boy, Lunch, Share
7.	Leftovers	Twelve, Baskets, Gather
8.	Twelve Baskets	Gather, Leftover

116 · The Signs of Our Saviour | © 2009 Striving Together Publications

Lesson Nine—Jesus Feeds Five Thousand

 # Teaching the Memory Verse

Romans 12:1

1   *I beseech you therefore, brethren, by the mercies of God, that ye present your bodies a living sacrifice, holy, acceptable unto God, which is your reasonable service.*

Print the "Crazy Clowns" cards. Glue the instruction sheet to the back of the "Crazy Clowns" sheet. Cut into four squares. Laminate for durability.

Display cards in front of class (Use a pocket chart, tape to wall, or hold in your hand). Choose one student to pick a "Crazy Clown." Have student read what is written on back side to class. The entire class will follow the instruction while repeating the verse. Repeat with the next seven cards.

Use companion flashcards found in Visual Resource Packet or images found on Ministry Resource CD.

Lesson Nine—Jesus Feeds Five Thousand

 # Object Lesson—God Can Use Me!

Materials Needed:
- Swiss Army knife

Lesson:

While showing the Swiss Army knife (closed) say, "Have you ever seen one of these? Do you know what it is called? What makes it different or special from a regular knife?"

Now open and show all the "tools." Each of these tools has a special job or use that is different from the others. Show the different tools and what they can do. (i.e. bottle opener, scissors, can opener etc.)

All of these tools are useful, all important and all different. You know what is really great? All of these tools are joined together in this one small device that you can keep in your pocket ready to be used whenever you need it.

Application:

This reminds me of our church! We are all different. We are all useful, and we are all important. Our job is just to be ready to be used whenever God asks.

So remember the Swiss Army knife, and remember that each Christian is important and has special abilities that God wants to be used for Him.

Lesson Nine—Jesus Feeds Five Thousand

 ## Craft—Fish

Getting It Together

1   Memory verse template located on the ministry resource CD

Paint
Glue
Scissors

Per student:
2   paper plates
1   wiggly craft eye

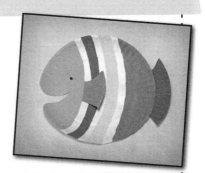

Putting It Together

1. Paint the paper plate any fish color
2. Cut a smiley face into the paper plate
3. Glue the wiggly eyes to the paper plate
4. Cut out the fins from the edging of the second paper plate
5. Glue the fins to the paper plate
6. Glue verse around the fish.

Seeing It Together

The fish will remind the students that God is faithful!

 ## Additional Resources

Find the following items on the Ministry Resource CD:
- Coloring Page (for younger children)
- Activity Page (for older children)
- Student Take-Home Paper
- PowerPoint Presentation

Suggested Classroom Schedule

Before Class	Complete attendance record. Provide students with coloring pages/activity pages.
Opening	Welcome
Prayer	Prayer requests and praise reports from the children
Song Time	
Memory Verse	Hebrews 12:2
Song Time	
Object Lesson	Blinders for Humans?
Bible Lesson	Jesus Walks on Water
Application/Invitation	Help saved students apply lesson. Invite unsaved students to receive Christ.
Snack	Walking on Water Cupcakes
Review Game/ Questions	STOP
Craft	Foot Bookmark
Closing	Announcements and Prayer Distribute take-home papers.

Lesson Ten Overview

Jesus Walks on Water
Theme—Always keep your eyes on Jesus.

Scripture
Matthew 14:22–33

Memory Verse
Hebrews 12:2—*"Looking unto Jesus the author and finisher of our faith; who for the joy that was set before him endured the cross, despising the shame, and is set down at the right hand of the throne of God."*

Lesson Outline

Introducing the Story
In the story we will learn today, we again find the disciples on a boat. But this time Jesus is not with them in the boat. Once again, a storm suddenly occurs. And, once again, Jesus demonstrates His loving care for them and His powerful authority over nature.

Telling the Story
1. **The Disciples in a Storm without Jesus** (vv. 22–24, *Mark 1:35*)
2. **Jesus Arrives, Walking on Water!** (vv. 25–27, *Psalm 46:1*)
3. **Peter's Daring Request and Step of Faith** (vv. 28–29, *James 2:18b*)
4. **Jesus Rescues Peter from Drowning** (vv. 30–31, *Hebrews 12:2*)
5. **Jesus Calms the Storm and is Worshiped** (vv. 32–33)

Applying the Story
We must keep our eyes on Jesus and have complete faith in Him!

10 Lesson Ten

Jesus Walks on Water

Theme: Always keep your eyes on Jesus.

Scripture

Matthew 14:22–33

22 And straightway Jesus constrained his disciples to get into a ship, and to go before him unto the other side, while he sent the multitudes away.

23 And when he had sent the multitudes away, he went up into a mountain apart to pray: and when the evening was come, he was there alone.

24 But the ship was now in the midst of the sea, tossed with waves: for the wind was contrary.

25 And in the fourth watch of the night Jesus went unto them, walking on the sea.

26 And when the disciples saw him walking on the sea, they were troubled, saying, It is a spirit; and they cried out for fear.

27 But straightway Jesus spake unto them, saying, Be of good cheer; it is I; be not afraid.

28 And Peter answered him and said, Lord, if it be thou, bid me come unto thee on the water.

29 And he said, Come. And when Peter was come down out of the ship, he walked on the water, to go to Jesus.

30 But when he saw the wind boisterous, he was afraid; and beginning to sink, he cried, saying, Lord, save me.

31 And immediately Jesus stretched forth his hand, and caught him, and said unto him, O thou of little faith, wherefore didst thou doubt?

32 And when they were come into the ship, the wind ceased.

33 Then they that were in the ship came and worshipped him, saying, Of a truth thou art the Son of God.

Memory Verse

Hebrews 12:2

"Looking unto Jesus the author and finisher of our faith; who for the joy that was set before him endured the cross, despising the shame, and is set down at the right hand of the throne of God."

Lesson Ten—Jesus Walks on Water

Teacher's Checklist

Snack Suggestion

To help the students remember today's lesson, prepare cupcakes with blue frosting (to represent water). Place a *Sour Patch Kid* candy on top (to represent Peter walking on water toward Jesus).

- ❑ Read Matthew 14:22–33 daily
- ❑ Study Lesson Ten
- ❑ Prepare snack—cupcakes, frosting, and Sour Patch Kids
- ❑ Gather for object lesson—horse blinders (or picture of horse blinders)
- ❑ Print and cut out "STOP" review game from Ministry Resource CD
- ❑ Print this week's memory verse (Hebrews 12:2) from the Ministry Resource CD
- ❑ Purchase for craft—construction paper and white paper
- ❑ Print for craft—foot verse template from the Ministry Resource CD
- ❑ Print for craft—foot template from the Ministry Resource CD
- ❑ Gather for craft—crayons
- ❑ Print and duplicate Coloring Pages or Activity Pages on the Ministry Resource CD (one per student)
- ❑ Print and duplicate Take-Home Paper on the Ministry Resource CD (one per student)

Bible Lesson

Scripture: Matthew 14:22–33

INTRODUCING THE STORY

As you have noticed, many things happened during the life and ministry of Jesus near the Sea of Galilee. Like many people today, Jesus and His disciples lived near the water. Can you remember the two miracles we learned about recently which took place on boats? The first was the great catch of fish with Peter. The second was when Jesus was asleep on a boat and then calmed the storm. In addition to these, we have learned about miracles that occurred just after Jesus departed from a boat on the Sea of Galilee.

Have you ever gone on a boat ride? Maybe some of you have been in a fishing boat with a friend or relative on a lake. Some may have been in a raft on a river. Maybe you rode on a ferryboat to an island. A few may have even been on a giant cruise ship on the ocean.

In the story we will learn today, we again find the disciples on a boat. But this time Jesus is not with them in the boat. Once again, a storm suddenly occurs. And, once again, Jesus demonstrates His loving care for them and His powerful authority over nature.

THE STORY

1. The Disciples in a Storm without Jesus (vv. 22–24)

Last week we learned about how Jesus multiplied a boy's lunch of a few fishes and bread and fed over five thousand people! Immediately after that miracle, Jesus told His disciples to go over to the other side of the Sea of Galilee. As the disciples got into the boat, Jesus instructed the rest of the crowd that it was also time for them to return to their own homes.

Do you think the disciples may have wondered why Jesus did not go with them? Usually they traveled together. But Jesus had something more important to do. He needed to pray. Jesus is a wonderful example to us today. Even though He has great wisdom, power, and love, He still needed to pray to His Father. This is one of many times when Jesus went away to pray to His Father alone. This verse in the first chapter of Mark is a good example:

Mark 1:35

35 And in the morning, rising up a great while before day, he went out, and departed into a solitary place, and there prayed.

While Jesus was praying alone on the top of the mountain, His disciples were on the sea. The sun had gone down, and it was now dark outside. The wind began to blow very hard. The waves began to rise and toss the disciples' boat around.

During the previous storm we learned about, the disciples went to Jesus when He was sleeping in the boat. They woke Him up, and He calmed the storm. Do you think they wished that Jesus were with them in the boat during this storm?

2. Jesus Arrives, Walking on Water! (vv. 25–27)

Even though Jesus was not physically with the disciples at that moment, He knew exactly where they were. He knew all about their problem, and He was able to help them. This is a good lesson for us to remember. Even though Jesus is away from us in Heaven, He is still able to see us, know us, and help us!

Psalm 46:1

1 God is our refuge and strength, a very present help in trouble.

Does your teacher mark you "present" when you attend school? What does the teacher call it when you are not in class because you are sick or on vacation? "Absent!" Does the Bible say, in Psalm 46:1, that God is our "absent help" or our "present help"? He is our "present help" when we are in trouble! Even better than present, He is "very present!"

The disciples were surprised when Jesus appeared from out of the dark night, walking on the water. Waves were crashing and splashing all around, but He was walking as normally as you or I might walk down the hallway at home. At first the disciples did not know it was Jesus. They thought it was a spirit walking toward them. Maybe they thought this meant it was their time to die in the middle of this storm.

When Jesus was close enough for them to hear, He said, "It is I; be not afraid." Jesus said this because He knew they were afraid. I am sure that the disciples breathed a sigh of relief when they realized it was Jesus!

3. Peter's Daring Request and Step of Faith (vv. 28–29)

Peter asked Jesus if he could join Him out on the waves. Even asking this question showed that Peter had faith in Jesus. He believed that Jesus could enable him to do something that, in his own strength, he could not do. You see, Peter was no stranger to the Sea of Galilee. He knew that no man could walk on water by his own power.

Jesus said to Peter, "Come." If requesting to come onto the water showed that Peter had faith, then actually stepping out of the boat showed that Peter had great faith. Our faith in Jesus always needs to be followed with actions. For example, if you have faith that He can save someone, then you will act by witnessing to him or her. Or, if you have faith that He will bless your obedience to your parents, then you will act by obeying them. If you have faith that He will provide for your needs, then you will act by giving Him an offering.

That is why the song says, "trust *and* obey." First comes the faith, then comes the action. Our faith in God is shown to Him and to others through our actions.

James 2:18b

18b …I will shew thee my faith by my works.

4. Jesus Rescues Peter from Drowning (vv. 30–31)

Even though Peter started out with great faith, he did make one mistake. We can learn from his mistake. Peter took his eyes off of Jesus. Instead of keeping his eyes on Jesus, as he walked toward Him, Peter looked at the waves. Those waves caused fear and doubt in Peter's heart, and because of his loss of faith in Jesus, he began to sink.

We must remember to keep our eyes on Jesus throughout our lives. Sometimes we will be tempted to focus on things around us as Peter did, instead of focusing on Jesus. Someone might focus on a bully at school. Another student might focus on something difficult happening at home. Some children might focus their attention on a health problem in their lives or in the life of someone they love. It is okay to be aware of these things. But they must never become the focus of our attention. Our attention…our focus…our eyes must always stay on Jesus!

Hebrews 12:2

2 *Looking unto Jesus the author and finisher of our faith; who for the joy that was set before him endured the cross, despising the shame, and is set down at the right hand of the throne of God.*

As Peter began to sink, he called out to the Lord. Jesus reached out His hand and helped Peter stay on top of the waves. Jesus does not want us to doubt or fail, but when we do, we can know that He is still there, and He will not let us "drown." Jesus is patient and merciful with us as He was with Peter. When we feel that we have failed Him or disappointed Him, we must humbly allow Him to help us, as He reaches out in help and love.

5. Jesus Calms the Storm and Is Worshiped (vv. 32–33)

After rescuing Peter, Jesus helped him into the boat. As they stepped inside the boat, the wind immediately stopped. It was very similar to the other time when Jesus calmed the storm; only this time, He did not even need to say a single word! This shows us once again the great authority that Jesus has over nature. He did not need to tell the wind to calm with His words. He only needed to decide it should become calm in His mind, and it was done. Only Jesus has this power!

The disciples worshiped Jesus for the great power He demonstrated. And they called Him something very important. The disciples, for the first time in the book of Matthew, called Jesus "the Son of God" (verse 33). They continued to call Jesus God's Son after this. This miracle is important because it helped the disciples understand who Jesus really is.

APPLYING THE STORY

Just as Peter could not walk on water by himself, there are things that you and I cannot do, without Jesus' help. We cannot love others, obey the Bible, witness for Him, or grow in character, without Jesus' help. To receive Jesus' help, we must keep our eyes on Him.

But since we cannot see Jesus physically, how can we "keep our eyes on Him"? We should keep our attention—our "mind's eye"—focused on

Him. Have you ever visualized something in your mind? (Consider asking the students to close their eyes and visualize something they would enjoy experiencing. Maybe a hot fudge sundae, or a front row seat at a sporting event.) You didn't see the thing physically, but you focused your attention on that thing, and in your mind, you could see it.

How do you focus your mind's eye on Jesus? By reading His Word each day, by memorizing verses, by praying daily, and by attending church faithfully. These are ways to keep our eyes on Jesus.

Review Game/Questions

"STOP"

Materials Needed
"STOP" and "point" circles from the Ministry Resource CD.

Instructions
Print the "STOP" circles on red cardstock and print the "point" circles on green cardstock. Cut out all the circles.

Place all circles in a bag. Ask the class a review question. When a student answers a question correctly, he/she will then reach into the bag.

- If the student pulls out a red "STOP," his/her turn is over and no points are awarded.
- If the student pulls out a green circle with points, he/she can stop and keep the points on the circle or the student can continue reaching in the bag, as long as, he/she is pulling out green circles.
- The student can stop at anytime and keep the total points drawn.
- If the student has a green circle and wants to continue but pulls a "STOP," he/she loses all the points for that turn.

The team with the most points wins.

1. Why did Jesus go up into a mountain?
   Answer: To pray

2. What was the weather like out on the sea?
   Answer: Stormy wind and waves

3. How did Jesus appear to the disciples?
   Answer: Jesus was walking on the sea.

4. What did the disciples think they saw?
   Answer: A spirit

5. How did the disciples feel when they first saw Jesus walking on the sea?
   Answer: They were afraid.

6. Who asked if he could walk out to Jesus?
   Answer: Peter

7. What made Peter afraid?
   Answer: The strong winds

8. What made Peter begin to sink?
   Answer: Doubt and fear

9. What did Peter do when he began to sink?
   Answer: He cried to the Lord to save him.

10. Did Peter walk on water in his own power?
    Answer: No, he needed God's power.

Lesson Ten—Jesus Walks on Water

Teaching the Memory Verse

Hebrews 12:2

2   *Looking unto Jesus the author and finisher of our faith; who for the joy that was set before him endured the cross, despising the shame, and is set down at the right hand of the throne of God.*

Print visuals for Hebrews 12:2 from the Ministry Resource CD.

If you have ever been in a race, you know how important it is to keep your eyes on the finish line or the goal. Looking back or getting distracted by what's around us will only cause us to slow down, get off course, or worse, trip and fall. The Bible likens our life as a race and Jesus is our goal. We need to keep our eyes on Him!

"Looking unto Jesus the author and finisher of our faith"—Our race starts with Jesus and by Him it is completed. Jesus is the One who will award the prize to them that are faithful unto death.

"who for the joy that was set before him"—The joy was that of fulfilling the will of the Father.

"endured the cross, despising the shame"—Jesus suffered all the pain and shame of dying on the Cross for our sins.

"and is set down at the right hand of the throne of God"—Jesus didn't stay dead; He arose and has His rightful place next to God the Father. Praise the Lord!

On this earth we may have many obstacles in our race, but if we're patient and keep our eyes on Jesus, we too will be rewarded in Heaven.

Use companion flashcards found in Visual Resource Packet or images found on Ministry Resource CD.

Lesson Ten—Jesus Walks on Water

Object Lesson—Blinders for Humans?

Materials Needed:
Blinders that a horse would wear (or a picture of one)

Lesson:
Show the students the blinders. Does anyone know what these are? Yes, they are blinders, sometimes called blinkers or winkers!

What are they used for? They are put on a horse basically to keep the horse focused on what is in front of it. Since the horse can't see everything in its peripheral vision, it keeps the horse from becoming distracted or scared.

Application:
Do you know who else needs blinders? We do! Sometimes we can get distracted by the things in this world and that means we take our eyes off Jesus. When we pass out a tract, when we read our Bible in public, or when we take a stand for Christ, we may get scared by what other people think of us.

Let this be a lesson to us to keep our eyes focused on the Lord and His Word.

Lesson Ten—Jesus Walks on Water

Craft—Foot Bookmark

Getting It Together

Black construction paper
White paper
Crayons
Glue
Scissors

Per student:
1. foot verse template for each student located on the Ministry Resource CD
1. foot template located on the Ministry Resource CD

Putting It Together

1. Print and cut out the verse template of the foot onto white paper.
2. Color the verse page.
3. Using the provided template of the foot located on the Ministry Resource CD, cut out enough feet for each student on black construction paper.
4. Glue the foot verse onto the black foot.

Seeing It Together

Encourage each student to walk daily with the Lord in Bible reading, prayer, and soulwinning.

Additional Resources

Find the following items on the Ministry Resource CD:
- Coloring Page (for younger children)
- Activity Page (for older children)
- Student Take-Home Paper
- PowerPoint Presentation

The Signs of Our Saviour | © 2009 Striving Together Publications

Suggested Classroom Schedule

Before Class	Complete attendance record. Provide students with coloring pages/activity pages.
Opening	Welcome
Prayer	Prayer requests and praise reports from the children
Song Time	
Memory Verse	Psalm 9:1
Song Time	
Object Lesson	Show and Tell
Bible Lesson	Jesus Heals a Blind Man
Application/Invitation	Help saved students apply lesson. Invite unsaved students to receive Christ.
Snack	Carrots and dip
Review Game/ Questions	Blind Vote
Craft	Megaphone
Closing	Announcements and Prayer Distribute take-home papers.

Lesson Eleven Overview

Jesus Heals a Blind Man

Theme—I can tell others what Jesus has done for me.

Scripture
John 9:1–7; 9:16–38

Memory Verse
Psalm 9:1 —"I will praise thee, O LORD, with my whole heart; I will shew forth all thy marvellous works."

Lesson Outline

Introducing the Story
Jesus' disciples thought that anytime something bad happened to someone, it meant that person had committed some terrible sin. But at the beginning of today's story, Jesus corrected their way of thinking.

Telling the Story
1. **A Man Who Was Born Blind** (vv. 1–5, Philippians 1:12)

2. **Jesus Heals the Blind Man's Eyes** (vv. 6–8)—Flash Card 11.1

3. **The Pharisees Question the Man and His Parents** (vv. 16–23, Luke 14:5) —Flash Card 11.2

4. **A Good Answer and a Good Question** (vv. 24–34, Psalm 126:2–3)

5. **The Man Believes in and Worships Jesus** (vv. 35–38, Psalm 107:1) —Flash Card 11.3

Applying the Story
Even though this man had only been healed for a very few minutes, he was able to speak to others about what Jesus Christ had done for him.

11 Lesson Eleven

Jesus Heals a Blind Man

Theme: I can tell others what Jesus has done for me.

Scripture

John 9:1–7; 16–38

1   And as Jesus passed by, he saw a man which was blind from his birth.
2   And his disciples asked him, saying, Master, who did sin, this man, or his parents, that he was born blind?
3   Jesus answered, Neither hath this man sinned, nor his parents: but that the works of God should be made manifest in him.
4   I must work the works of him that sent me, while it is day: the night cometh, when no man can work.
5   As long as I am in the world, I am the light of the world.
6   When he had thus spoken, he spat on the ground, and made clay of the spittle, and he anointed the eyes of the blind man with the clay,
7   And said unto him, Go, wash in the pool of Siloam, (which is by interpretation, Sent.) He went his way therefore, and washed, and came seeing.
16 Therefore said some of the Pharisees, This man is not of God, because he keepeth not the sabbath day. Others said, How can a man that is a sinner do such miracles? And there was a division among them.
17 They say unto the blind man again, What sayest thou of him, that he hath opened thine eyes? He said, He is a prophet.
18 But the Jews did not believe concerning him, that he had been blind, and received his sight, until they called the parents of him that had received his sight.
19 And they asked them, saying, Is this your son, who ye say was born blind? how then doth he now see?
20 His parents answered them and said, We know that this is our son, and that he was born blind:
21 But by what means he now seeth, we know not; or who hath opened his eyes, we know not: he is of age; ask him: he shall speak for himself.

Memory Verse

Psalm 9:1
"I will praise thee, O LORD, with my whole heart; I will shew forth all thy marvellous works."

Lesson Eleven—Jesus Heals a Blind Man

22 *These words spake his parents, because they feared the Jews: for the Jews had agreed already, that if any man did confess that he was Christ, he should be put out of the synagogue.*

23 *Therefore said his parents, He is of age; ask him.*

24 *Then again called they the man that was blind, and said unto him, Give God the praise: we know that this man is a sinner.*

25 *He answered and said, Whether he be a sinner or no, I know not: one thing I know, that, whereas I was blind, now I see.*

26 *Then said they to him again, What did he to thee? how opened he thine eyes?*

27 *He answered them, I have told you already, and ye did not hear: wherefore would ye hear it again? will ye also be his disciples?*

28 *Then they reviled him, and said, Thou art his disciple; but we are Moses' disciples.*

29 *We know that God spake unto Moses: as for this fellow, we know not from whence he is.*

30 *The man answered and said unto them, Why herein is a marvellous thing, that ye know not from whence he is, and yet he hath opened mine eyes.*

31 *Now we know that God heareth not sinners: but if any man be a worshipper of God, and doeth his will, him he heareth.*

32 *Since the world began was it not heard that any man opened the eyes of one that was born blind.*

33 *If this man were not of God, he could do nothing.*

34 *They answered and said unto him, Thou wast altogether born in sins, and dost thou teach us? And they cast him out.*

35 *Jesus heard that they had cast him out; and when he had found him, he said unto him, Dost thou believe on the Son of God?*

36 *He answered and said, Who is he, Lord, that I might believe on him?*

37 *And Jesus said unto him, Thou hast both seen him, and it is he that talketh with thee.*

38 *And he said, Lord, I believe. And he worshipped him.*

The Signs of Our Saviour | © 2009 Striving Together Publications

Lesson Eleven—Jesus Heals a Blind Man

Teacher's Checklist

- ☐ Read John 9:1–7; 9:16–38 daily
- ☐ Study Lesson Eleven
- ☐ Flashcards 11.1–11.3
- ☐ Prepare snack—carrots and dip
- ☐ Contact students to participate in "Show and Tell."
- ☐ Print this week's memory verse (Psalm 9:1) from the Ministry Resource CD.
- ☐ Purchase for craft—Styrofoam cups, ribbon, and foam decorations
- ☐ Print for craft—verse template from the Ministry Resource CD
- ☐ Gather for craft—crayons, scissors, and glue
- ☐ Print and duplicate Coloring Pages or Activity Pages on the Ministry Resource CD (one per student)
- ☐ Print and duplicate Take-Home Paper on the Ministry Resource CD (one per student)

Snack Suggestion

Since carrots are often associated with good eyesight, serve carrots and ranch dip as today's snack.

The Signs of Our Saviour | © 2009 Striving Together Publications

Lesson Eleven—Jesus Heals a Blind Man

Bible Lesson

Scripture: John 9:1–7; 16–38

INTRODUCING THE STORY

Have you ever wondered why difficult and painful things happen to good people? Maybe someone you love has lost their job. Maybe you know a very nice person who became sick, and maybe they became so ill that he or she went to Heaven. Why does God allow these things to occur?

The disciples of Jesus thought they knew the answer to this question. They thought that anytime something bad happened to someone, it meant that person had committed some terrible sin to deserve the difficulty. But at the beginning of today's story, Jesus corrected their way of thinking.

THE STORY

1. A Man Who Was Born Blind (vv. 1–5)

Teacher's Note

The Pool of Siloam was the only permanent water source for the city of Jerusalem in the first century. It was fed by the waters of the Gihon Spring diverted through Hezekiah's Tunnel.

When the disciples met a man near the pool of Siloam who was born blind, they asked Jesus what he did to deserve the blindnes or what his parents did wrong. Jesus said that his blindness was not the man's or his parents' fault. He explained that God, His Father, allows some difficult things to occur in our lives simply so that He may receive glory through that circumstance.

God also allows bad things to happen so that people may hear about His Son Jesus. For example, because Stephen was stoned, Paul believed on Jesus. And because Paul went to jail, the Philippian jailor and his family were saved.

Paul explained that the things that occur in our lives, both good and bad, happen so that more people will hear the message of Jesus.

> **Philippians 1:12**
>
> 12 But I would ye should understand, brethren, that the things which happened unto me have fallen out rather unto the furtherance of the gospel;

This was also the case in the story of this blind man. Because of his blindness, Jesus would receive glory, and people would believe on Him and be saved later in the story.

136   The Signs of Our Saviour | © 2009 Striving Together Publications

2. Jesus Heals the Blind Man's Eyes (vv. 6–8)

Flash Card 11.1

Jesus used a method to heal this man that might seem strange to us. Jesus spat on the ground (I do not suggest you do this at church or school!). Then Jesus mixed up the spit with the dirt on the ground. What did it make? Mud! He took the mud and wiped it on the man's eyes. (Has one of your parents ever put medicine that you did not want on a hurt that you had?) Then Jesus told the man to wash the mud off of his eyes in a nearby pool of water (like a fountain in a public place), which was called the Pool of Siloam.

Jesus healed many blind people during His ministry. And it is interesting to read that He chose to heal them in many different ways. See some of the ways Jesus healed the blind:

- Matthew 9:27–30—Jesus healed two blind men by touching their eyes.
- Matthew 12:22—Jesus healed a blind man by casting a demon out of him.
- Mark 8:22–25—Jesus healed a blind man by spitting on his eyes and then touching them.
- Matthew 15:30—Jesus healed many blind people on a mountain.
- Mark 10:52—Jesus healed a blind man by only speaking to him.
- Matthew 20:30–34—Jesus healed two more blind men by touching their eyes.
- Matthew 21:14—Jesus healed many blind people inside the Temple.

What can we learn from this? We learn that the miracles were not based on a magical formula, or being in the right place, or using a particular method. The one common reason all of these blind people were healed was Jesus! Always remember that the miracles and power of Jesus are not based on some fancy trick or good luck. They are based on His great power as God's Son.

3. The Pharisees Question the Man and His Parents (vv. 16–23)

Flash Card 11.2

The Pharisees were leaders in the Jewish religion. They did not like Jesus because He stole the attention away from them. They criticized Jesus for doing kind things and performing miracles on the Sabbath day, which was a day of rest for the Jews. The Pharisees said Jesus was not of God, because He healed on the Sabbath. Jesus explained to them at a different time that His Father never meant that they could not do good things for others on this day of rest.

Lesson Eleven—Jesus Heals a Blind Man

Luke 14:5

5   *And answered them, saying, Which of you shall have an ass or an ox fallen into a pit, and will not straightway pull him out on the sabbath day?*

First the Pharisees asked the formerly blind man what his opinion of Jesus was. He answered, "He is a prophet" (verse 17).

Then the Pharisees asked his parents, "How then doth he now see?" The parents were afraid of these Jewish leaders. So all they said was that they knew it was their son, and they knew he used to be blind, but they did not know how he was healed. They said, "He is of age. Ask him."

Then the Pharisees asked the man again what he thought of Jesus. They tried to get him to say that Jesus was a sinner, since He did this thing on the Sabbath day.

4. A Good Answer and a Good Question (vv. 24–34)

The man said he wasn't sure whether Jesus was a sinner or not. But what he did know was, "I was blind; now I see." This is a good answer! He would learn more about Jesus later, but for now he could at least emphasize what Jesus had done for him. As soon as the blind man could see, he was ready to tell others. How long do we need to be saved before we witness? We should witness right away!

Psalm 126:2–3

2   *Then was our mouth filled with laughter, and our tongue with singing: then said they among the heathen, The LORD hath done great things for them.*

3   *The LORD hath done great things for us; whereof we are glad.*

We can learn a lesson from the blind man who was now healed. You may not know how to explain everything from the Bible. But if you can explain that Jesus loves you, died on the Cross for you, and has done good things for you, then you can be like this man.

After this good answer, the Pharisees actually asked the man how this miracle occurred again. This was the fourth time they asked! Weren't they listening? They kept hearing answers that they did not believe. So the man asked them a question of his own. He said something like this: "Why do you keep asking about Jesus? Do you want to be His disciples, too?" What a great question!

138   *The Signs of Our Saviour* | © 2009 Striving Together Publications

5. The Man Believes in and Worships Jesus (vv. 35–38)

Flash Card 11.3

Of course, the Pharisees were very angry about this man's desire to honor Jesus. They told him that he was not allowed to come back into the Temple unless he changed his mind about Jesus (verse 34). Do you think he was disappointed? If you were blind for your entire life, and now because of a wonderful man named Jesus you could see, would it bother you what some grumpy, boring men thought of you? I don't think so!

Leaving the Pharisees, the man found Jesus. Jesus asked him, "Do you believe on the Son of God?" Could you guess the man's answer? "Lord, I believe." The man then bowed himself down at Jesus' feet, thanking Him for the wonderful thing He had done. Have you thanked Jesus for the good things He has done for you?

Psalm 107:1

1   *O give thanks unto the LORD, for he is good: for his mercy endureth for ever.*

APPLYING THE STORY

Even though this man had only been healed for a very few minutes, he was able to speak to others about what Jesus Christ had done for him. There were many things he did not know (verse 25). But there was "one thing" he did know: Jesus had touched and healed him. He was not an expert in religion, but he was an expert in what happened to his own eyes!

Teacher's Note

The words found in Psalm 107:1 are given, word-for-word, five places in the Psalms (106:1, 107:1, 118:1, 29, 136:1), as well as in 1 Chronicles 16:34 and Ezra 3:11.

Sometimes we think witnessing for Jesus is more difficult than it really is. Speaking to others about Jesus really only requires telling them what we know has happened to us. Have you asked Jesus to be your Saviour? If you have, then you know how to tell someone else what happened to you. Did He take your sins away? Do you pray to Him? If so, then you can tell others what it means to have a relationship with Jesus Christ. You can tell others what Jesus has done for you.

Can you give an example of something Jesus would like for you to share with someone else?

Lesson Eleven—Jesus Heals a Blind Man

Review Game/Questions

Blind Vote

Materials Needed
None

Instructions
Divide the class in half. Ask one side (Team One) a question. After the student answers, have the other side (Team Two) bow their heads and close their eyes. Team Two votes on whether they think the answer is correct by raising their hands. Workers count how many hands are raised and how many are not. Give the correct answer. Award a point for each correct vote. Repeat with the other side. The team with the most points wins.

1. How long had this man been blind?
   Answer: Since birth

2. What did the disciples want to know about his blindness?
   Answer: If he was blind because of his sin or the sin of his parents

3. Why did Jesus say he was blind?
   Answer: "that the works of God should be made manifest in him"

4. How did Jesus heal the blind man?
   Answer: He spat on the ground, made mud, and then anointed the eyes of the blind man.

5. Jesus told the blind man to go wash in a pool. What was the name of the pool?
   Answer: Siloam

6. Why did the Pharisees say that Jesus was not of God?
   Answer: Because He did not keep the Sabbath

7. What did the Pharisees ask the parents?
   Answer: How can he see?

8. What did the man's parents say to the Pharisees?
   Answer: Ask him yourself; he is an adult.

9. How long do we need to be saved before we can be a witness for Jesus?

   Answer: Right after we are saved

10. After Jesus heard that the man was cast out of the synagogue, what did He ask him?

    Answer: Do you believe in the Son of God?

Teaching the Memory Verse

Psalm 9:1

1   *I will praise thee, O LORD, with my whole heart; I will shew forth all thy marvellous works.*

Print verse flashcards from the Ministry Resource CD. Have four students come to the front of the class and hold visuals. Have the class say the verse several times.

Option #1—Divide the class into four groups. Have them go to the four corners of the classroom. Give them five minutes to come up with a cheer for this verse.

Option #2—Take a few minutes and allow the students to give a testimony of what God has done in their life. Encourage them to tell their testimony this week to someone who doesn't go to church.

Use companion flashcards found in Visual Resource Packet or images found on Ministry Resource CD.

Lesson Eleven—Jesus Heals a Blind Man

Object Lesson—Show and Tell

Before Class:
Call three or four students and ask them to bring something to class on Sunday for "Show and Tell."

Lesson:
"Show and Tell" was always a fun time for me when I was in school. We have a few students who have some things they want to share with us during this "Show and Tell" time today. Allow the students whom you called to show and tell what they brought.

Application:
Did you know that, as Christians, we all have something to show and tell all the time? Every day our lives should "show" that there is something different (from the world) about us. Then, we should look for opportunities to "tell" others about Jesus and what He did for us on Calvary.

We don't have to wait for someone to call us to participate in "Show and Tell." Let's remember to participate in "Show and Tell" every day!

Lesson Eleven—Jesus Heals a Blind Man

Craft—Megaphone

Getting It Together

Ribbon
Fast-drying glue
Foam decorations
Scissors

Per student:
1   foam cup
1   verse template located on the Ministry Resource CD

Putting It Together

1. Start by printing off the verse template.
2. Glue the verse to the lip of the foam cup. (When gluing items to a foam cup, we recommend using a fast drying glue.)
3. Cut the bottom of the cup out, smoothing the edges out with your fingers.
4. Glue the ribbon around the lip of the cup, being careful to not cover up the verse on the lip of the cup.
5. Decorate the cup with foam decorations or construction paper cut outs.

Seeing It Together

Encourage the students to tell the good news of Jesus to others.

Additional Resources

Find the following items on the Ministry Resource CD:
- Coloring Page (for younger children)
- Activity Page (for older children)
- Student Take-Home Paper
- PowerPoint Presentation

The Signs of Our Saviour | © 2009 Striving Together Publications

Suggested Classroom Schedule

Before Class	Complete attendance record. Provide students with coloring pages/activity pages.
Opening	Welcome
Prayer	Prayer requests and praise reports from the children
Song Time	
Memory Verse	Ephesians 5:20
Song Time	
Object Lesson	Learning to Be Thankful
Bible Lesson	Jesus Heals Ten Lepers
Application/Invitation	Help saved students apply lesson. Invite unsaved students to receive Christ.
Snack	Fruit Roll Ups by the Foot
Review Game/ Questions	Give? or Take!
Craft	Thank You Cards
Closing	Announcements and Prayer Distribute take-home papers.

Lesson Twelve Overview

Jesus Heals Ten Lepers
Theme—Remember to thank Jesus for what He does.

Scripture
Luke 17:11–19

Memory Verse
Ephesians 5:20—"Giving thanks always for all things unto God and the Father in the name of our Lord Jesus Christ;"

Lesson Outline

Introducing the Story
Today's story is about ten lepers, whom Jesus met while traveling to Jerusalem.

Telling the Story

1. **Ten Lepers Standing in the Distance** (vv. 11–12, Leviticus 13:45–46)

2. **The Lepers Ask for Mercy and Are Healed** (vv. 13–14, Psalm 69:16, Ephesians 2:4)

3. **The Man Glorifies God** (v. 15, James 1:17, Psalm 29:2)

4. **The Man Thanks Jesus** (v. 16, Psalm 92:1, Colossians 3:15)

5. **Jesus' Question and Concern** (vv. 17–19, Romans 1:21, 2 Timothy 3:2)

Applying the Story
If you and nine of your friends had just received a wonderful miracle from Jesus, and if only one of you remembered to thank Jesus, would you be that one?

> Patty—
> You are now on Lesson 12 :)

...elve

...pers

...Jesus for what He does.

Memory Verse

Ephesians 5:20
"Giving thanks always for all things unto God and the Father in the name of our Lord Jesus Christ;"

...erusalem, that he passed through the

...ge, there met him ten men that were

...said, Jesus, Master, have mercy on us.
...o them, Go shew yourselves unto the
...they went, they were cleansed.
...he was healed, turned back, and with

..., giving him thanks: and he was

...ere not ten cleansed? but where are

18 There are not found that ...... to give glory to God, save this stranger.
19 And he said unto him, Arise, go thy way: thy faith hath made thee whole.

Lesson Twelve—Jesus Heals Ten Lepers

 Teacher's Checklist

- ❏ Read Luke 17:11–19 daily
- ❏ Study Lesson Twelve
- ❏ Purchase snack—Fruit Roll Ups by the Foot
- ❏ Gather for object lesson—candy and a gift bag
- ❏ Memory verse (Ephesians 5:20) from the Visual Resource Packet
- ❏ Purchase for craft—construction paper and glitter
- ❏ Gather for craft—crayons, scissors, and glue
- ❏ Print and duplicate Coloring Pages or Activity Pages on the Ministry Resource CD (one per student)
- ❏ Print and duplicate Take-Home Paper on the Ministry Resource CD (one per student)

 Snack Suggestion

To reinforce the fact that one leper ran back to thank Jesus, consider serving *Fruit Roll Ups by the Foot*.

146   The Signs of Our Saviour | © 2009 Striving Together Publications

Lesson Twelve—Jesus Heals Ten Lepers

Bible Lesson

Scripture: Luke 17:11–19

INTRODUCING THE STORY

Do you remember a time when you were lonely? You may have felt lonely because your family and friends were doing something else, or had gone somewhere. Maybe you were attending a new school or church where you did not know anyone. No one likes to feel alone.

Leprosy is a disease that we read about in the Bible. Some people in other countries still have leprosy today. It is a terrible disease that involves great pain and more sores on your skin than you can probably imagine. People who had leprosy were called lepers. Today's story is about ten lepers, who met Jesus as He was traveling to Jerusalem, passing through Samaria and Galilee.

> **Use an Object**
>
> **Talcum Powder and Cotton Balls**
> Dab talcum powder dots on students to represent leprosy.

THE STORY

1. Ten Lepers Standing in the Distance (vv. 11–12)

One of the worst things about leprosy was that if you had it, no one wanted to be anywhere near you. People feared that those with leprosy were contagious and that if they got too close, they would catch the terrible disease themselves. So, those with leprosy had to call out "Unclean! Unclean!" as they walked through the streets.

The first time leprosy is mentioned in the Bible is in Leviticus 13. In that chapter, God gave the Jewish people guidelines for what someone must do if they got the disease of leprosy.

> **Act It Out**
>
> **Lepers**
> Have students call out, "Unclean! Unclean!" when you mention the lepers.

Leviticus 13:45–46

45 *And the leper in whom the plague is, his clothes shall be rent, and his head bare, and he shall put a covering upon his upper lip, and shall cry, Unclean, unclean.*

46 *All the days wherein the plague shall be in him he shall be defiled; he is unclean: he shall dwell alone; without the camp shall his habitation be.*

The Signs of Our Saviour | © 2009 Striving Together Publications

These lepers were forced to leave their city. Due to their disease, they ended up living in a group together. By this time in Jesus' ministry, nearly everyone had heard about the amazing and wonderful things He had done. When these lepers saw Jesus coming, they had hope that He might cleanse them.

2. The Lepers Ask for Mercy and Are Healed (vv. 13–14)

The lepers asked Jesus for mercy. Why mercy? Because all men are sinners, and we all deserve punishment from Jesus. These lepers knew they had done sinful things in their lives and they did not deserve for Jesus to cleanse them. We can be thankful not only that Jesus showed mercy to them, but also that He is willing to show mercy to us, even today!

Teacher's Note

Mercy:
"compassion or forgiveness shown toward someone whom it is within one's power to punish or harm"—New Oxford American Dictionary

Psalm 69:16

16 Hear me, O LORD; for thy lovingkindness is good: turn unto me according to the multitude of thy tender mercies.

The Bible says that God is "rich in mercy." This means that He will never run out of mercy. He has mercy for anyone who needs it—and that's everyone!

Ephesians 2:4

4 But God, who is rich in mercy, for his great love wherewith he loved us,

Here on earth, whenever people ask Jesus for mercy, He will give it to them (John 6:37). If you have not yet asked Jesus to be your Saviour, to forgive your sins and to take you to Heaven one day, you may make the decision to ask Him for mercy today!

Jesus told them to go and show themselves to the priest because Jewish lepers who thought they had recovered from their leprosy were to do this. They had been instructed by Moses to go see a priest, who would check their bodies and make sure they were truly healed. This had to be done before they could go back home or to work.

As these men followed Jesus' instructions and left, they were suddenly healed! They walked away, headed to see the priest and knew that they were cleansed completely. Imagine how happy they must have been!

3. The Man Glorifies God (v. 15)

As the ten men walked toward the part of town where they knew the priest would be, one of them turned around to thank Jesus for what He had done. The other nine kept going, excited to get to the priest and then back to their family, friends, or jobs.

The Bible says that this one man, who was from Samaria, "glorified God." This means that with great joy, he let everyone around him know that this blessing was from God. All of us have good things in our lives, but we do not always glorify God for them. Most people simply forget Who the source is for their healthy bodies, their loving family, their good church, and their home in Heaven.

James 1:17

1   *Every good gift and every perfect gift is from above, and cometh down from the Father of lights, with whom is no variableness, neither shadow of turning.*

Glorifying God means: 1) realizing the blessings come from Him and 2) letting everyone know how great He is! This leper, who was now cleansed, glorified God. Do we have things for which we should glorify God? (Allow students to give examples.) We are taught in the Bible that we should give God the glory He deserves.

Psalm 29:2

2   *Give unto the LORD the glory due unto his name; worship the LORD in the beauty of holiness.*

4. The Man Thanks Jesus (v. 16)

The man did not only glorify God. He also bowed down at the feet of Jesus and thanked Him for cleansing him. Glorifying God is publicly telling others what He has done. Thanking God is privately telling Him, "Thank You!"

Lesson Twelve—Jesus Heals Ten Lepers

Psalm 92:1

1   *It is a good thing to give thanks unto the LORD, and to sing praises unto thy name, O most High:*

Colossians 3:15

15   *And let the peace of God rule in your hearts, to the which also ye are called in one body; and be ye thankful.*

> **Teaching Tip**
>
> Make a list of things for which we can be thankful. Take answers from students and write them on the chalk or dry erase board.

Being thankful is more than an action. It's an attitude! Remember, you can thank Jesus for things at all times of the day anywhere in the world. Whenever you see something to be thankful for, make it a habit to thank Jesus right then and there for what He did. If we wait, we might forget. Who knows, maybe the other nine lepers intended to come back and thank Jesus later, but they didn't.

5. Jesus' Question and Concern (vv. 17–19)

It is interesting that when they had leprosy, all ten spoke to Jesus, asking for His help and mercy. But once they were healed, only one took the time to thank Jesus. This is the way most of us are. We complain about things we don't have, but we don't thank God for things we do have. We remember to pray when there's a problem, but we forget to pray when things are going well for us.

Jesus asked the question, "Were there not ten cleansed? but where are the nine?" Jesus was concerned that most of these men were not thankful.

How seriously do you think God takes the sin of being unthankful? There are two famous chapters in the New Testament that include lists of horrible sins. These chapters are Romans 1 and 2 Timothy 3. These chapters include sinful people such as murderers (Romans 1:29), haters of God (Romans 1:30), blasphemers, and those that are unholy (2 Timothy 3:2). Notice that both of these lists also include the sin of being unthankful:

Romans 1:21

21   *Because that, when they knew God, they glorified him not as God, neither were thankful; but became vain in their imaginations, and their foolish heart was darkened.*

Lesson Twelve—Jesus Heals Ten Lepers

2 Timothy 3:2

2 *For men shall be lovers of their own selves, covetous, boasters, proud, blasphemers, disobedient to parents, unthankful, unholy,*

APPLYING THE STORY

If you and nine of your friends had just received a wonderful miracle from Jesus, and if only one of you remembered to thank Jesus, would you be that one?

Let's share some things for which we can thank Jesus! We should take some time in class to bow our heads and thank Him for these good things He has done for us. But we should also take some time at home and in other places to thank Him.

Review Game/Questions

Give? or Take!

Instructions
Print visuals for "Give? or Take!" from the Ministry Resource CD. Cut the word sheet into four squares and glue to black construction paper. Cut the construction paper into four squares. Laminate for durability. Cut out point circles and glue them to black construction paper. Cut out the circles.

To Play
Put the points in a bag. Hold the "Give? or Take!" cards in your hands. Make sure the students can't see the words!

Divide the class into teams. Beginning with Team 1, ask a review question. If student answers correctly, he/she may reach into the bag (without looking) and pull out one circle. Announce to the class the point value of that circle.

The Signs of Our Saviour | © 2009 Striving Together Publications

151

Lesson Twelve—Jesus Heals Ten Lepers

Now have that same student pick a card from your hand to determine who gets all those points. If a "give" is chosen, then Team 1 gives Team 2 those points. If the chosen card is a "take", then Team 1 gets to keep those points. The team with the most points wins.

1. As Jesus went to Jerusalem, what two places did He pass through?
   Answer: Samaria and Galilee

2. When Jesus entered the village, how many lepers did He meet?
   Answer: Ten

3. What is leprosy?
   Answer: A terrible skin disease

4. When someone came near a leper, what would the leper have to do?
   Answer: Call out "unclean"

5. What did the lepers say to Jesus?
   Answer: Master, have mercy on us

6. What did Jesus tell them to do?
   Answer: Go show themselves to the priests.

7. As they went to the priests, what happened to the lepers?
   Answer: They were cleansed.

8. How many lepers gave glory to the Lord?
   Answer: Only one

9. Where was the thankful leper from?
   Answer: Samaria

10. What did this one leper do physically?
    Answer: He fell on his face at Jesus' feet and gave thanks.

Lesson Twelve—Jesus Heals Ten Lepers

 # Teaching the Memory Verse

Ephesians 5:20

20 Giving thanks always for all things unto God and the Father in the name of our Lord Jesus Christ;

Print verse from the Ministry Resource CD on cardstock. Cut along the dotted lines. Use a pocket chart or the chalk tray to display one word strip at a time. Have students repeat each phrase several times, then add the next word strip.

After the students have said the entire verse a few times, remove the word strips, shuffle them, and give them to a student. Time the student to see how long it takes to place the strips in correct order on the pocket chart. Then, say the whole verse again as a class.

Variation One:
Give each word strip to a different student. When you say, "Go!" they can work together as a team to put the verse in order.

Variation Two:
Print two sets of the verse and divide the class into two teams. The teams can then compete against each other to put the scrambled strips in the correct order.

Use companion flashcards found in Visual Resource Packet or images found on Ministry Resource CD.

The Signs of Our Saviour | © 2009 Striving Together Publications

Lesson Twelve—Jesus Heals Ten Lepers

Object Lesson—Learning to Be Thankful

Materials Needed:
- Bite size candy for class
- 10 snack size candy bars
- 1 Large candy bar
- 1 Gift bag with tissue

Before class:

Put the ten snack size candy bars in the gift bag. Write the following instructions on slips of paper for every student in class. Put them in a bowl. On one slip of paper write, "Congratulations: You are the grand prize winner! Listen for me to announce the grand prize winner. Then come forward. If ANYONE asks you to share, you MUST give them one of the candy bars found inside, even if it means you will have none left for yourself."

On ten of the slips of paper, write, "Someone will be announced as a grand prize winner. Once the person has been given his prize, go to him and ask him to share it with you. When he does, do not say ANYTHING. Do NOT say thank you or anything else. Take the candy and return to your seat. If you say anything after he shares his prize with you, you will lose it."

On the remaining slips of paper, write, "Something interesting is going to happen today. Watch carefully. Do not make any comments until I say so."

Tell the class:

"You are not allowed to show your slip of paper to anyone. Do not talk to anyone about it. Follow the instructions on your slip of paper—exactly." Now announce to the class, "Will the Grand Prize Winner please come forward?" Let the student look in the bag and present him or her with the large candy bar.

Application/Discussion Questions:
- Did anyone say thank you for the candy?
- How did you feel that no one said "thank you"? Were you upset?
- How would you have felt had someone said "thank you"?
- Did any of you receiving the candy feel badly about accepting it without expressing your thanks?

Let's all remember to express our gratitude this week!

Craft—Thank You Cards

Getting It Together

Construction paper
Glue
Scissors
Glitter
Various other decorations

Putting It Together

Have each child make thank you cards to Jesus, pastor, or parents. Let each child decorate the thank you cards however they would like.

Seeing It Together

Encourage the students to have a gratitude attitude.

Additional Resources

Find the following items on the Ministry Resource CD:
- Coloring Page (for younger children)
- Activity Page (for older children)
- Student Take-Home Paper
- PowerPoint Presentation

Suggested Classroom Schedule

Before Class	Complete attendance record. Provide students with coloring pages/activity pages.
Opening	Welcome
Prayer	Prayer requests and praise reports from the children
Song Time	
Memory Verse	1 Peter 5:7
Song Time	
Object Lesson	The Strength of the Lord
Bible Lesson	Jesus Raises His Friend Lazarus
Application/Invitation	Help saved students apply lesson. Invite unsaved students to receive Christ.
Snack	Graveyard Hot Dogs
Review Game/ Questions	Questions and Answers
Craft	Lazarus Boy
Closing	Announcements and Prayer Distribute take-home papers.

Lesson Thirteen Overview

Jesus Raises His Friend Lazarus
Theme—Jesus cares about me and my family.

Scripture
John 11:1–5, 11–14, 17, 20–23, 32–45

Memory Verse
1 Peter 5:7— "Casting all your care upon him; for he careth for you."

Lesson Outline
Introducing the Story
Today's story includes a family that had two sisters and one brother. When the brother died, Jesus came to the sisters. He showed His love and care for their family, and He surprised everyone with what He did next.

Telling the Story
1. **Jesus' Friends: Mary, Martha, and Lazarus** (vv. 1–11, John 15:13–14)

2. **Is Lazarus Dead or Just Sleeping?** (vv. 11–19, 1 Thessalonians 4:13–14)

3. **Martha and Mary Share Broken Hearts with Jesus** (vv. 20–36, Romans 12:15, Matthew 11:28–30)

4. **Removing the Stone from the Grave** (vv. 37–41)

5. **Jesus Prays and Calls Lazarus out of the Grave** (vv. 41–45, 1 John 5:14, 1 Corinthians 15:52)

Applying the Story (1 Peter 5:7)
You cannot always tell what Jesus is doing, why He is doing it, or exactly when He will do something next. But you can always know that He cares!

13 Lesson Thirteen

Jesus Raises His Friend Lazarus
Theme: Jesus cares about me and my family.

Scripture

Memory Verse

1 Peter 5:7
"Casting all your care upon him; for he careth for you."

John 11:1–5, 11–14, 17, 20–23, 32–45

1   Now a certain man was sick, named Lazarus, of Bethany, the town of Mary and her sister Martha.
2   (It was that Mary which anointed the Lord with ointment, and wiped his feet with her hair, whose brother Lazarus was sick.)
3   Therefore his sisters sent unto him, saying, Lord, behold, he whom thou lovest is sick.
4   When Jesus heard that, he said, This sickness is not unto death, but for the glory of God, that the Son of God might be glorified thereby.
5   Now Jesus loved Martha, and her sister, and Lazarus.
11 These things said he: and after that he saith unto them, Our friend Lazarus sleepeth; but I go, that I may awake him out of sleep.
12 Then said his disciples, Lord, if he sleep, he shall do well.
13 Howbeit Jesus spake of his death: but they thought that he had spoken of taking of rest in sleep.
14 Then said Jesus unto them plainly, Lazarus is dead.
17 Then when Jesus came, he found that he had lain in the grave four days already.
20 Then Martha, as soon as she heard that Jesus was coming, went and met him: but Mary sat still in the house.
21 Then said Martha unto Jesus, Lord, if thou hadst been here, my brother had not died.
22 But I know, that even now, whatsoever thou wilt ask of God, God will give it thee.
23 Jesus saith unto her, Thy brother shall rise again.
32 Then when Mary was come where Jesus was, and saw him, she fell down at his feet, saying unto him, Lord, if thou hadst been here, my brother had not died.

Lesson Thirteen—Jesus Raises His Friend Lazarus

33 When Jesus therefore saw her weeping, and the Jews also weeping which came with her, he groaned in the spirit, and was troubled,

34 And said, Where have ye laid him? They said unto him, Lord, come and see.

35 Jesus wept.

36 Then said the Jews, Behold how he loved him!

37 And some of them said, Could not this man, which opened the eyes of the blind, have caused that even this man should not have died?

38 Jesus therefore again groaning in himself cometh to the grave. It was a cave, and a stone lay upon it.

39 Jesus said, Take ye away the stone. Martha, the sister of him that was dead, saith unto him, Lord, by this time he stinketh: for he hath been dead four days.

40 Jesus saith unto her, Said I not unto thee, that, if thou wouldest believe, thou shouldest see the glory of God?

41 Then they took away the stone from the place where the dead was laid. And Jesus lifted up his eyes, and said, Father, I thank thee that thou hast heard me.

42 And I knew that thou hearest me always: but because of the people which stand by I said it, that they may believe that thou hast sent me.

43 And when he thus had spoken, he cried with a loud voice, Lazarus, come forth.

44 And he that was dead came forth, bound hand and foot with graveclothes: and his face was bound about with a napkin. Jesus saith unto them, Loose him, and let him go.

45 Then many of the Jews which came to Mary, and had seen the things which Jesus did, believed on him.

Lesson Thirteen—Jesus Raises His Friend Lazarus

 # Teacher's Checklist

- ❑ Read John 11:1–45 daily
- ❑ Study Lesson Thirteen
- ❑ Prepare Snack—graveyard hot dogs
- ❑ Gather for object lesson—box with heavy contents
- ❑ Memory verse (1 Peter 5:7) from the Visual Resource Packet
- ❑ Print "Questions and Answers" game from Ministry Resource CD.
- ❑ Purchase for memory verse—2 twelve-inch balloons, fishing line, 12 clothes pins, straight pins, and permanent markers
- ❑ Purchase for craft—Coflex bandages
- ❑ Print boy template for craft from the Ministry Resource CD.
- ❑ Print verse template for craft from the Ministry Resource CD.
- ❑ Gather for craft—crayons, scissors, and glue
- ❑ Print and duplicate Coloring Pages or Activity Pages on the Ministry Resource CD (one per student)
- ❑ Print and duplicate Take-Home Paper on the Ministry Resource CD (one per student)

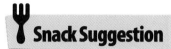 **Snack Suggestion**

Graveyard Hot Dogs
Wrap bread dough around hot dogs to represent grave cloths. Bake 10 minutes at 350.

Lesson Thirteen—Jesus Raises His Friend Lazarus

Bible Lesson

Scripture: John 11:1–5, 11–14, 17, 20–23, 32–45

INTRODUCING THE STORY

Do you have one or more brothers or sisters? How many? What are the blessings (and burdens, though not too many) of having brothers or sisters? Are there unique blessings or burdens for having older brothers or sisters? What about younger sisters or brothers?

Today's story includes a family that had two sisters and one brother. This family had a terrible thing happen. The brother got very sick and then died. But this family had a very special friend, the Lord Jesus Christ. When their brother died, Jesus came to His friend's sisters. He showed His love and care for their family, and He surprised everyone with what He did next.

THE STORY

1. Jesus' Friends: Mary, Martha, and Lazarus (vv. 1–11)

> **Use an Object**
>
> **Bath Tissue**
> Wrap a child loosely with bath tissue to represent Lazarus in grave clothes.

In the city of Bethany lived two sisters named Mary and Martha. These sisters had a brother named Lazarus. Jesus and His disciples often went to Bethany for ministry and sometimes even for some rest. One time in Bethany, Jesus enjoyed fellowship with this family in their home and shared a meal prepared by Martha (Luke 10: 38–42).

If Jesus were here on earth today, would you like Him to be one of your friends? Would you like Him to come to your home for dinner? What would you have to eat?

Do you think that if He were here today, He would choose you as one of His friends? You may not think so, but the Bible tells us that He has already chosen each of us as His friends. He explained to His disciples that He has shown Himself to be our Friend by laying down His life for us on the Cross. And we can show ourselves to be His friends by our obedience to Him.

John 15:13–14

13 Greater love hath no man than this, that a man lay down his life for his friends.

14 Ye are my friends, if ye do whatsoever I command you.

2. Is Lazarus Dead or Just Sleeping? (vv. 11–19)

The Bible says in the beginning of chapter 11 that Lazarus was sick. Martha and Mary had sent messengers from Bethany to tell Jesus about their sick brother, so that He might come and heal him. But then Lazarus died. The disciples did not know this, but Jesus did. He knew everything (John 18:4)!

His disciples got confused when Jesus said they needed to go where Lazarus was because he was asleep. They thought to themselves, "If someone's sick, don't they need their sleep?" But Jesus was not referring to that kind of sleep. Jesus used the word "sleep" to describe the fact that Lazarus was dead. Why would Jesus have used the word "sleep"? Because He planned to raise Lazarus from the dead! Since Lazarus' eyes were closed but would open again in just a few days, Jesus said he was asleep.

The Bible continues to use the term "sleep" to describe what happens when a Christian's body dies, because death is only temporary! Jesus will raise our bodies up again one day, just as He would raise Lazarus.

1 Thessalonians 4:13–14

13 *But I would not have you to be ignorant, brethren, concerning them which are asleep, that ye sorrow not, even as others which have no hope.*

14 *For if we believe that Jesus died and rose again, even so them also which sleep in Jesus will God bring with him.*

3. Martha and Mary Share Broken Hearts with Jesus (vv. 20–36)

When Martha heard that Jesus was on His way to Bethany, she ran to meet Him (verse 20). She explained that He was too late. However, Jesus explained to Martha that her brother would live again. Martha thought Jesus meant many years later, when God would raise all dead believers. But Jesus was referring to just a few minutes from then!

Next, Mary came to meet Jesus. She said the exact same thing to Him as her sister did, "Lord, if thou hadst been here, my brother had not died."

The Bible tells us that Jesus saw these sisters weeping and their friends weeping. He asked Martha and Mary to take Him to where Lazarus' body was. Then we read one of the shortest verses in the Bible, "Jesus wept" (verse 35).

Lesson Thirteen—Jesus Raises His Friend Lazarus

When people are sad, one of the ways to show them love is to weep along with them.

Romans 12:15

15   *Rejoice with them that do rejoice, and weep with them that weep.*

Jesus always cares about those having a difficult time. Jesus invites those who are sad, lonely, tired, confused, or hurting to Himself. He promises that He will personally give comfort and rest. He is a wonderful, tender, loving Saviour!

Matthew 11:28–30

28   *Come unto me, all ye that labour and are heavy laden, and I will give you rest.*

29   *Take my yoke upon you, and learn of me; for I am meek and lowly in heart: and ye shall find rest unto your souls.*

30   *For my yoke is easy, and my burden is light.*

> **Teacher's Note**
>
> Mark 16:1–6 records the wonderful occasion when the stone was rolled away from Jesus' tomb.

4. Removing the Stone from the Grave (vv. 37–41)

Jesus and the sisters came to the grave where Lazarus' body lay. Most graves in those times were similar to caves. They were hollow places in the sides of rocky hills or mountains. Once someone's body was laid inside the cave, a heavy stone was rolled in front of the opening so that the person's body was closed-off inside the tomb (or grave).

Jesus told some of the people standing nearby to remove the stone from the grave. Can you think of another stone that was rolled away from a grave in the New Testament? Jesus' stone was rolled away from His grave, too!

5. Jesus Prays and Calls Lazarus out of the Grave (vv. 41–45)

As the stone was rolled away, Jesus began to look up toward Heaven and prayed to His Father. He said, "Father, I thank thee that thou hast heard me." Jesus knew and was thankful that His Father in Heaven could hear His prayers, even though they were far away.

162   The Signs of Our Saviour | © 2009 Striving Together Publications

Did you know that God can hear your prayers just as well? God always hears the prayers of His children.

1 John 5:14

14   *And this is the confidence that we have in him, that, if we ask any thing according to his will, he heareth us:*

Then Jesus said, "Lazarus, come forth." Immediately Lazarus came out of the grave. He was wrapped in fabric like a mummy. But when Jesus told them to loosen the material around him, everyone could see that Lazarus had been miraculously brought back to life!

Jesus had power over death then, and Jesus still has power over death today! Death couldn't keep Lazarus in the grave. Death couldn't keep Jesus in the grave. And even though our bodies may one day die, Jesus will still take us to Heaven and even raise those bodies up one day, just as He did for Lazarus!

1 Corinthians 15:52

52   *In a moment, in the twinkling of an eye, at the last trump: for the trumpet shall sound, and the dead shall be raised incorruptible, and we shall be changed.*

APPLYING THE STORY

The fact that Jesus wept (verse 35) shows that He cares about the things in our lives that concern us. If you or someone you love is sick, Jesus cares. If someone has hurt you, Jesus cares about it. If your family is having a difficult time, Jesus cares about that, too.

1 Peter 5:7

7   *Casting all your care upon him; for he careth for you.*

You cannot always tell what Jesus is doing, why He is doing it, or exactly when He will do something next. But you can always know that He cares!

He especially cares whether you know Him as your Saviour. If you have never asked Him to forgive your sins and be your Saviour, you may do so today, if you understand that He is God's Son who has power over death.

Lesson Thirteen—Jesus Raises His Friend Lazarus

Review Game/Questions

Questions and Answers

Instructions

Print the "Question" sheet on one colored paper and the "Answer" sheet on another color paper. Cut out. Pass out the questions to the students. Then pass out the answers to students.

Have students with the questions try to find the student who has the answer. When they have found their match, they may sit down. When everyone has found their match, have the students read their questions and then the answer.

To make it a bit more challenging, you can add some incorrect answer cards.

1. Name the three siblings from today's lesson.
   Answer: Martha, Mary, and Lazarus

2. Where did Lazarus and his sisters live?
   Answer: Bethany

3. What emotion did Jesus have toward Lazarus, Mary, and Martha?
   Answer: He loved them.

4. Mary and Martha went to Jesus to tell Him their brother was sick. How long did Jesus stay in the same place where He was?
   Answer: Two days

5. After Mary and Martha came to Jesus, where did He tell His disciples He wanted to go?
   Answer: Judaea

6. When Jesus said Lazarus was sleeping, what did that mean?
   Answer: He was dead.

7. When Jesus arrived, how long had Lazarus been in the grave?
   Answer: Four days

8. Which sister went out to meet Jesus?
   Answer: Martha

9. What emotion did Jesus show when He saw Mary and the Jews?
   Answer: Jesus wept.

10. What did Martha say when Jesus said to take away the stone?
    Answer: He stinketh.

11. What happened to many of the Jews that came with Mary after they had seen Lazarus raised from the dead?
    Answer: They believed on Jesus.

Teaching the Memory Verse

1 Peter 5:7

7 Casting all your care upon him; for he careth for you.

Materials Needed:
- At least twelve 12-inch balloons, light colors only
- Fishing line or thin string
- Clothespins
- Straight pin (Preferably the kind with a large bead at the end—this will be easier to hold.)
- Flashcard from Ministry Resource CD

Inflate 12 balloons. Write the reference on balloon 1. Write each word of the verse on the remaining 11 balloons with a black permanent marker (as large as you can). Attach fishing line to the front wall or chalkboard. Clothespin the balloons (in verse order) to the fishing line.

Turn to 1 Peter 5:7. Read together as a class. The word "care" here means worry. God wants us to give (cast) all our worries to Him. Why? Because He cares for us! Choose one student to come to the front and pop (with the straight pin) one of the balloons. Now have the class repeat the verse. Continue in this same manner until all the balloons are popped and the class can recite the verse without any help.

Lesson Thirteen—Jesus Raises His Friend Lazarus

 # Object Lesson—The Strength of the Lord

Materials Needed:
A box (or suitcase)—too heavy for your student to lift by himself but light enough for you and the student to lift.

Lesson:
Put the box in front of the class. Ask a student to come carry the box. When the student cannot lift it, say: "I think this box is too heavy to lift all by yourself. But I can help you, let me carry it with you." Then carry the box together.

Application:
The box represents the burdens we carry (list some that you know your students struggle with—i.e. dad needs a job, a loved one who is away from the Lord, a friend needs to be saved, family needs money to pay bills, etc. These burdens are hard to carry, but God doesn't want us to carry them, He wants us to give our burdens to Him. He can carry anything!

Lesson Thirteen—Jesus Raises His Friend Lazarus

Craft—Lazarus Boy

Getting It Together

Coflex bandages
Crayons
Scissors
Glue

Per student:
1 boy template located on the Ministry Resource CD
1 verse template located on the Ministry Resource CD

Putting It Together

1. Print and color the boy.
2. Print and color the verse, curling the ends to look like a scroll.
3. Cut small strips of coflex bandages, wrap them around the boy
4. Glue the verse template onto the hand of the boy.

Seeing It Together

Just as Jesus cared for Mary, Martha, and Lazarus, He cares for us, too!

Additional Resources

Find the following items on the Ministry Resource CD:

- Coloring Page (for younger children)
- Activity Page (for older children)
- Student Take-Home Paper
- PowerPoint Presentation

The Signs of Our Saviour | © 2009 Striving Together Publications

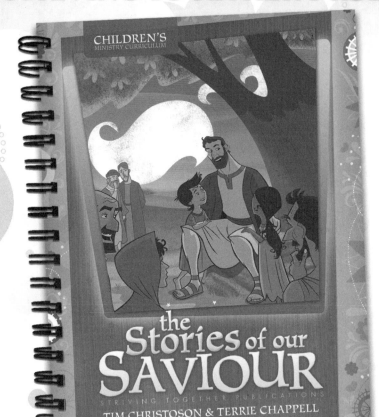